THÉRÈSE OF LISIEUX and MARIE OF THE TRINITY

THÉRÈSE of LISIEUX and MARIE of the TRINITY

The transformative relationship of Saint Thérèse of Lisieux
and her novice Sister Marie of the Trinity

PIERRE DESCOUVEMONT

Translated by
Alexandra Plettenberg-Serban

ALBA·HOUSE   NEW·YORK

SOCIETY OF ST. PAUL, 2187 VICTORY BLVD., STATEN ISLAND, NEW YORK 10314

ST PAULS

Thérèse of Lisieux and Marie of the Trinity
is a translation of
Une novice de Sainte Thérèse: Soeur Marie de la Trinité
(Souvenirs et témoignages présentés par Pierre Descouvemont
3rd edition, revised and improved)
Les Editions du Cerf
29, Boulevard Latour-Maubourg, Paris, 1993

Library of Congress Cataloging-in-Publication Data

Descouvemont, Pierre.
[Novice de Sainte Thérèse, soeur Marie de la Trinité, carmélite de
Lisieux. English]
Thérèse of Lisieux and Marie of the Trinity: the transformative relationship
of Saint Thérèse of Lisieux and her novice Sister Marie of the Trinity / Pierre
Descouvemont; translated by Alexandra Plettenberg-Serban.
  p.   cm.
ISBN 0-8189-0732-0
1. Marie de la Trinité, soeur, 1874-1944. 2. Thérèse, de Lisieux,
Saint, 1873-1897. 3. Carmelite Nuns — France — Biography. I. Title.
BX4705.M365D4713   1997
271'.971022 — dc21   97-20167
[B]   CIP

Produced and designed in the United States of America by the
Fathers and Brothers of the Society of St. Paul,
2187 Victory Boulevard, Staten Island, New York 10314,
as part of their communications apostolate.

ISBN: 0-8189-0732-0

Printing Information:

Current Printing - first digit	1	2	3	4	5	6	7	8	9	10

Year of Current Printing - first year shown

1997	1998	1999	2000	2001	2002	2003	2004	2005

I would like to express my deep gratitude
to Bernadette Frenzel, OSB.
This translation would not have reached publication
without her substantial collaboration.

Table of Contents

Introduction to the English Version xi

Translator's Note xiii

Abbreviations xv

Foreword: No! Life Is Not Sad! xvii

HOW DO WE KNOW ABOUT SR. MARIE OF THE TRINITY? xx

Family Tree of Thérèse Martin xxiii

Chapter One: A Life Full of Unknowns 1

I. BEFORE ENTRANCE INTO THE CARMEL OF LISIEUX (1874-1894) 1

A numerous family *1*

Settling in Paris *2*

An atmosphere of prayer *2*

Discovery of a vocation *3*

First contacts with Carmel *5*

In the Carmel of l'avenue de Messine *6*

Towards the Carmel of Lisieux *7*

II. IN THE CARMEL OF LISIEUX (1894-1944) 9

A) AT THE TIME OF THÉRÈSE 9

A great joy for Thérèse *10*

A difficult novice *11*

Taking of the Habit *14*

Spiritual accompaniment *15*

Family concerns *17*

The Holy Face *18*

Offering to Merciful Love *19*

Sr. Marie of the Trinity and of the Holy Face *20*

The profession 21
Novitiate meetings 24
Small means in the service of love 25
A great theologian 28
The atmosphere of the novitiate 30
Be always happy 31
A friendship becomes deeper 33
The separation begins 35
Brief encounters 36
The death of a saint 38
B) After the Death of Thérèse 40
1. In the radiance of Thérèse (1897-1923) 41
The memory of Thérèse in Carmel 42
Various works of the young nun 44
The mail 45
At the service of pilgrims 46
Daily life in the monastery 48
Depositions for the Processes 49
Some extraordinary events 50
A fervent disciple 51
A fresh fidelity 52
The celebrations at Lisieux 54
2. In the resemblance of the Holy Face (1923-1944) 55
A long Way of the Cross 55
A "little mama" and godmother for the Work of Fr. Brottier 56
Joy during hard times 58
The affection of Mother Agnes 59
The friendship of a Trappist 61
The end of Calvary 62

Chapter Two: The Testimony of Marie of the Trinity 65
A Profound Faith in the Love of God 65
Holy Scripture 65
The Holy Face 66
The Eucharistic Mystery 68
Joy on One's Face 71

MERCIFUL LOVE 74
A PROFOUND HUMILITY 78
AN AUDACIOUS CONFIDENCE 85
TO DO EVERYTHING OUT OF LOVE 89
TO PLEASE GOD 93
THE REWARD OF SUFFERING 95
A HEROIC LOVE 97
    Mortifications of the body 97
    A heroic obedience 98
    A perfect chastity 99
    An authentic poverty 100
    Faithfulness in little things 101
THE JOY OF SAVING SOULS 103
LOVING RELATIONSHIPS 105
    An unshakable patience 106
    "Love does not seek its own interest" 108
    Spiritual friendship 109
    Saying "thank you" 110
    The choice of the last place 110
    A total availability 111
    The discernment of the novice mistress 112
    The conduct of the novices towards
      Mother Marie de Gonzague 113
    To spend her heaven doing good on earth 115

Chapter Three: Secrets of a Heroic Joy 117
    Not to be appalled by one's miserable condition 118
    To love God as much as Thérèse did 120
    Love in little things 120
    The joy of loving 121
    To suffer without courage 123
    To suffer one minute at a time 124
    To save the world 125
    In the image of the Holy Face 125
    The sweet presence of Thérèse 127
    To help the scatterer of roses 128

An unchangeable confidence 129
An outlook full of hope 129

Conclusion 131

Appendix: Testimonial Documents 137
A) Five Series of Documents 137
  1. Counsels and Reminiscences *from
     the* Story of a Soul *(CSM)* 137
  2. *The deposition in the Bishop's Process (PO)* 138
  3. *The* Red Notebook *(CRM)* 139
  4. *The deposition in the Apostolic Process (PA)* 140
  5. *To these four documents is added another series of* Counsels
     and Reminiscences *which can be gleaned from the papers
     of Marie of the Trinity or from the writings concerning her.
     An issue of* Vie thérèsienne *printed a regrouping of
     twenty-seven of them (CSM 31-57)* 141
B) The Value of the Witness 142
C) Dating of the Reminiscences 143

Chronology of the Life of Sister Marie of the Trinity 145

Introduction to the English Version

On the occasion of the Centenary of Saint Thérèse of Lisieux in 1997, we English speaking readers get an opportunity for the very first time to study this Saint in a close relationship with someone other than her own sisters. It is to her youngest novice, Sister Marie of the Trinity, that Thérèse feels able to transmit her deepest thoughts in a language that is completely her own, simple and sometimes casual, matching the character of this "Parisian youth" who reminds us of Thérèse's own nature before her mother's death.

Marie of the Trinity was considered a "difficult and unruly person" by her religious community, just as Thérèse "passed almost unnoticed" among them. It is Thérèse who helps Marie transform the exuberance and impatience of her very nature into enthusiasm, into passionate and steady dedication in all her commitments into a love of God that enables her novice later on to lead an extraordinary life after Thérèse's death. Marie in return, with her great sensitivity and perception, but also her critical questioning, becomes a stimulus to Thérèse, a vessel for her teaching, a model for the path which she later names "the little way." Both women share a love for each other that nourishes their spiritual growth and leads to the transcendence of their entire relationship.

Today more than ever, we can profit from the study of this testimony since we live in a time of renewal and redefinition of religious communities and leadership, of rethinking the nature of any relationship. Thérèse redefines the role of the novice mistress and expands its boundaries far beyond its traditional scope. She understands that as a novice mistress she has to be Christlike, not only a teacher, but also a loving mother, compassionate friend, firm spiritual director and tender sister to her novices. We see here, how in every act, every gesture and every conversation she focuses completely on the needs and issues of the other person. Instead of interpreting this material for them, she takes and refocuses it towards the love of God, using her many artistic gifts to create tools for this purpose. In this way she always respects the possibilities of that person within the context of God's unique love.

We know from the testimonies after her death, that "by the time Thérèse died she had shaped her small group of five nuns along her own lines... and a few years afterwards the entire convent was remodelled in her image, which year by year shone forth more brightly. This metamorphosis was so unexpected, so difficult to accomplish, and so profound and enduring, that the nuns recognized it to be the first and greatest miracle after her passing" (Ida Friederike Goerres, *The Hidden Face*, p. 231).

I wish to take this opportunity to thank the author, Fr. Pierre Descouvemont, and Fr. Edmund C. Lane, S.S.P., of Alba House for their generous assistance and encouragement in the translation and publication of this book.

New York, April 15, 1997

Translator's Note

Supplementary notes are bracketed within the text or are footnotes, to distinguish them from the author's (now endnotes).
Supplementary material in the author's footnotes are in italics.

Le regard and its verb *regarder* are so central to Thérèsian
spirituality of the Holy Face, that these will be noted in the text
when relevant. *Le regard* means "look, gaze, glance" but also "the
whole face" or countenance.

I have used my own translation of Scripture in order to
render the author's given text, using the following abbreviations:

Esther	Esther	Mt	Matthew
Hos	Hosea	Lk	Luke
Is	Isaiah	Jn	John
Job	Job	Col	Colossians
2 Kings	2 Kings	Gal	Galatians
Song	Song of Songs	1 Pet	1 Peter
		Rev	Revelation

I have also added a Chronology of Sr. Marie of the Trinity.

ABBREVIATIONS

(* indicates works already translated)

A,B,C	*Les trois Manuscrits autobiographiques de Thérèse avec indication du folio, recto ou verso.* The three Autobiographical Manuscripts of Thérèse with indication of the folio, front or back.
ACL	*Archives du carmel de Lisieux.* (Lisieux Carmel Archives).
Agnes	*Billets de soeur Marie de la Trinité à Mère Agnès de Jésus, publiés dans VT 85 et 89.* (Notes of Sister Marie of the Trinity to Mother Agnes of Jesus).
Annales	*Les Annales de Sainte Thérèse de Lisieux,* Lisieux, *revue mensuelle.* (Annals of Saint Thérèse of Lisieux).
BT	*La Bible avec Thérèse de Lisieux,* Cerf/DDB, 1979. (The Bible with Thérèse of Lisieux).
CG	*Correspondance générale de Thérèse,* 2 t., Cerf/DDB, 1972 et 1974.* (*General Correspondence,* 2 volumes).
CJ	*Carnet Jaune de Mère Agnès de Jésus,* publié dans DE.* ("Yellow Notebook" of Mother Agnes of Jesus).
CRM	*Carnet Rouge rédigé par soeur Marie de la Trinité et publié dans VT 74 et 75.* ("Red Notebook" edited by Sister Marie of the Trinity).
CSM	*Conseils et Souvenirs relatés par soeur Marie de la Trinité et publié dans VT 73 et 77.* (*Counsels and Reminiscences* related by Sister Marie of the Trinity).
DE	*Derniers Entretiens de Thérèse,* Cerf/DDB, 1971. (*Last Conversations* of Saint Thérèse of the Child Jesus and the Holy Face).
Germaine	*Lettres de soeur Marie de la Trinité à soeur Germaine Leconte, du carmel d'Angers, et publiées dans VT 87 et 88.* (Letters of Sister Marie of the Trinity to Sister Germaine Leconte, of the Angers Carmel).

HA 99   *Histoire d'une Ame*, édition 1899.
          (*Story of a Soul*, 1899 edition; the 1898 edition has been
          translated).

LT   *Lettres de Thérèse selon la numérotation de la Correspondance
          générale* (CG).*
          (Letters of Thérèse according to the numbering of the
          General Correspondence).

NPPA   *Notes préparatoires au Procès apostolique* (ACL).
          (Preparatory notes for the Apostolic Process).

Obituary *Circulaire nécrologique de soeur Marie de la Trinité* (ACL).
          (Obituary letter of Sister Marie of the Trinity).

PA   *Procès apostolique* (1915-1917), Rome, Teresianum, 1976.
          (Apostolic Process, 1915-1917).

PN   *Poésies de Thérèse selon la numérotation de l'édition critique*,
          Cerf/DDB, 1979.
          (Poems of Thérèse according to the numbering in the critical
          edition).

PO   *Procès de l'Ordinaire* (1910-1911), Rome, Teresianum, 1973.
          (The Bishop's Process, 1910-1911).

Pri   *Prières composées par Thérèse* à paraître chez Cerf/DDB.
          (Prayers composed by Thérèse).

RP   *Recréations pieuses de Thérèse* publiées dans *Théâtre au Carmel*,
          Cerf/DDB, 1985.
          ("Pious Recreations" of Saint Thérèse of the Child Jesus).

VT   *Vie thérèsienne*, Lisieux, *revue trimestrielle*.
          (*Thérèsian Life*, Lisieux).

VTL   *Visage de Thérèse de Lisieux*, Lisieux, 2 t., 1961.*
          (*The Face of Thérèse of Lisieux*, two volumes, 1961).

No!
Life Is Not Sad!

The title of this Foreword should not give a false impression. Sr. Marie of the Trinity and of the Holy Face suffered very much. During the last years of her life she became more and more disfigured by lupus [tuberculosis of the skin]. At the end, it took more than two hours to redo her bandages every morning. But until the last moment she heroically lived "the spirituality of the smile" which she had learned at the beginning of her religious life from Sr. Thérèse of the Child Jesus.

Sr. Marie of the Trinity was the youngest novice of Thérèse. Having entered the Carmel of Lisieux on June 16, 1894, two months before her twentieth birthday, she profited from the spiritual counsels of her novice mistress for three years and rapidly became her friend and her most ardent disciple.

The entrance of the young nun was not without impact on the dynamism of Thérèse herself. The presence in the novitiate of this Parisian *titi*[1] rejuvenated the atmosphere and Thérèse quickly found in her a resonant instrument able to vibrate intensely with the great spiritual intuitions which were being born in her own heart. The novice responded very spontaneously with great vivacity to the teachings that she heard. It can be said without exaggeration that without the presence of Sr. Marie of the Trinity in the Lisieux Carmel, Thérèse would not have been able to so vividly articulate and live the originality of her "little

---

[1] Lit.: street urchin; a child with street-smarts (trans.).

doctrine," as she loved to call it. It is well known that one understands much better what one has the opportunity to teach!

Even beyond this, Sr. Marie of the Trinity contributes some very precious insights into our knowledge of Thérèse. Smart and sensitive,[2] she easily took note of everything she saw and heard, so her testimony quickly became very important after Thérèse's death, when every memory of her life counted.

During the canonization Process it was said that Thérèse had her four "evangelists": John, Luke and Matthew in the persons of her three Carmelite sisters — Pauline, Marie and Céline — and Mark in the person of Marie of the Trinity. Her testimony does in fact resemble what has come down to us from the spokesman of the apostle Peter; her accounts are extremely vivid. While the Martin sisters were interested in the more developed teachings of Thérèse, Sr. Marie of the Trinity preferred very life-like flashes, including all the comparisons that her novice mistress invented to make herself better understood.

Unfortunately, this testimony is not well known. Although the old editions of Story of a Soul contain appendices of large extracts from the Counsels and Reminiscences of Thérèse's novices — especially those of Sr. Marie of the Trinity — today they can be found only in the two massive volumes of the canonization Process, published in 1973 and 1976, and in a series of articles edited by Sr. Cécile, of the Carmel in Lisieux, and published in many issues of the journal Vie thérèsienne.

We thought it opportune to give to the public at large the possibility of getting to know what Marie of the Trinity has left for us concerning this "child beloved to the world," as Pope Pius XI called St. Thérèse. This comprises the second chapter of the present work, which will undoubtedly capture the reader's interest. All of us depend on the excellent critical work done by Sr. Cécile; in full accord with her, we have chosen to present this

---

[2] Lit: like a fly on the wall.

testimony in the simplest manner possible, a simplicity which would mirror the same simplicity of Thérèse and her novice.

The first chapter presents the life story and the personality of the witness. This biography will allow a better understanding of certain remarks made by Sr. Thérèse to a novice who retained a certain "street urchin" character from her Parisian childhood. We have also included in this chapter some very personal counsels that Thérèse gave to her, which would sound ridiculous if generalized to others. The reader will also find some very fresh "first-hand" accounts of life in the Lisieux Carmel during the 50 years following Thérèse's death. What events took place in this little country Carmel!

The third and last chapter shows that the Carmelite was not content to just remember the example and the counsel she received; she put them into practice. Particularly sensitive to what Thérèse taught her about the art of being happy in all circumstances, she made an effort to smile at all times, even when half of her face could no longer do it! Sr. Marie of the Trinity and of the Holy Face began at a very early age to contemplate the disfigured Holy Face of her Lord. She knew that she could continue to please him with the leprotic face that she herself had at the end of her life, a face she thought gave her the privilege of being like the Holy Face of her Beloved.

She also remembered one of the last words that Thérèse had spoken to her, one day in the infirmary when the young nun had given vent to her pain at seeing her suffer:

"Oh! how sad life is!" Marie of the Trinity had said to her.

"No, no! Life is not sad," Thérèse had replied. "Were you[3] to say, 'exile is sad,' I would understand you. People make a mistake to

---

[3] Even though they belonged to the family of the Carmelite community and became intimate friends, Thérèse and Marie as religious always addressed one another in conversation and in writing as "you," employing the formal second person *vous*, "thou" — customary for expressing respect — rather than the informal or familiar *tu*. In the 19th century it was common to speak even to one's parents as *vous*. Thérèse's prayers often address God as *tu*. Exceptions to this usage will be noted in the text (trans.).

give the name of 'life' to things that must end. Only to heavenly things, things that never end, can you give this real name. In this context, life is not sad but happy, very happy!" (CSM, 30).

HOW DO WE KNOW ABOUT SR. MARIE OF THE TRINITY?

a) Through some autobiographical notes drawn up in March 1904, with the permission of Mother Agnes. Towards the end of 1894, without doubt after her taking of the habit (December 18), the young novice had shared with Thérèse her desire to put in writing the great graces of her life, so as not to forgot them. She thought that the rereading of these notes would do her good. *"Beware of doing any such thing!"* responded Thérèse; *"besides, you can't do it without permission, and I advise you not to ask for it. For myself, I would never want to write my life story without a special order to do so, an unasked-for order at that. It is more humble never to write about oneself. The great graces of life, like those of a vocation, can't be forgotten; they will serve you better by being recalled to mind than by being reread on paper."*[4] Thérèse didn't suspect that the following month she herself would receive from Mother Agnes the order to write her own childhood recollections! [...]

The fact still remains that in 1904, an "order," or at least an explicit permission, of Mother Agnes of Jesus, then prioress, came to release the pen of Marie of the Trinity, and what she wrote is very modest. Her text is entitled *The Story of My Vocation.* The author was principally attentive to note the providential circumstances that permitted her youthful desire to be realized, that of having as her friend a woman who was also a saint.

b) Through the sermon given by Father J.-B. Charles, chaplain of the Institute of St. Geneviève d'Asnières, the day of Marie

---

[4] PO, p. 468.

of the Trinity's taking of the veil at the Carmel of Lisieux (May 7, 1896). It contains several interesting details about her younger days.

c) Through the documents described in an appendix to this volume, where the former novice furnishes us with the whole of her testimony on Thérèse, providing us with many details relative to her own life.

d) Through the obituary letter of Marie of the Trinity that Mother Agnes drafted in 1944, in collaboration with Sr. Marie-Emmanuelle. To a large extent they used the autobiographical notes of 1904.

e) Through the obituary letter of Sr. Marguerite-Agnes, the little sister of Marie of the Trinity, who died at the Visitation in Caen on October 27, 1964.

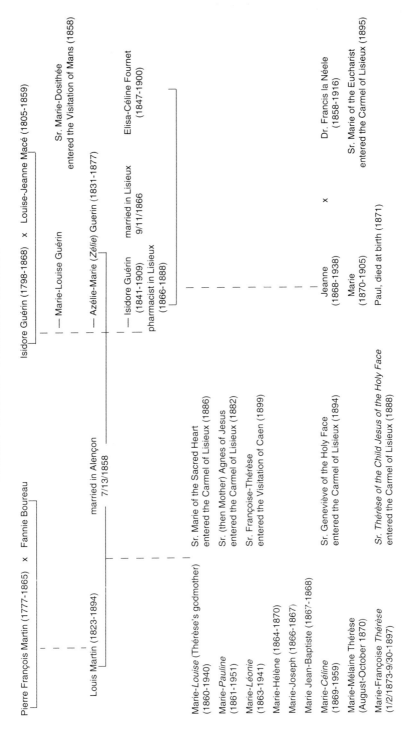

FAMILY TREE OF THÉRÈSE MARTIN

Pierre François Martin (1777-1865) × Fannie Boureau

Isidore Guérin (1798-1868) × Louise-Jeanne Macé (1805-1859)

— Marie-Louise Guérin

— Sr. Marie-Dosithée
entered the Visitation of Mans (1858)

Louis Martin (1823-1894)

married in Alençon
7/13/1858

— Azélie-Marie (*Zélie*) Guérin (1831-1877)

— Isidore Guérin
(1841-1909)
pharmacist in Lisieux
(1866-1888)

married in Lisieux
9/11/1866

×

Elisa-Céline Fournet
(1847-1900)

Jeanne
(1868-1938)

Dr. Francis la Néele
(1858-1916)

Marie
(1870-1905)

Sr. Marie of the Eucharist
entered the Carmel of Lisieux (1895)

Paul, died at birth (1871)

Marie-*Louise* (Thérèse's godmother)
(1860-1940)

Sr. Marie of the Sacred Heart
entered the Carmel of Lisieux (1886)

Marie-*Pauline*
(1861-1951)

Sr. (then Mother) Agnes of Jesus
entered the Carmel of Lisieux (1882)

Marie-*Léonie*
(1863-1941)

Sr. Françoise-Thérèse
entered the Visitation of Caen (1899)

Marie-Hélène (1864-1870)

Marie-Joseph (1866-1867)

Marie Jean-Baptiste (1867-1868)

Marie-*Céline*
(1869-1959)

Sr. Geneviève of the Holy Face
entered the Carmel of Lisieux (1894)

Marie-Mélanie Thérèse
(August-October 1870)

Marie-Françoise *Thérèse*
(1/2/1873-9/30/1897)

Sr. *Thérèse of the Child Jesus of the Holy Face*
entered the Carmel of Lisieux (1888)

THÉRÈSE OF LISIEUX and MARIE OF THE TRINITY

CHAPTER ONE

A Life Full of Unknowns

I. BEFORE ENTRANCE INTO THE CARMEL OF LISIEUX
(1874-1894)

A numerous family

Marie-Louise Castel was born on August 12, 1874, in St.-Pierre-sur-Dives in Calvados, where her father was then a teacher in the elementary school. She was baptized the following day.

Her mother, Leontine le Comte, came from a village near Lisieux, St.-Martin-de-la-Lieue. Marie-Louise was brought there to a wet nurse right after her birth, to one of her maternal aunts. She did not return to her mother's house until she was four years old. There was plenty of work to be done at home. Marie-Louise had three older sisters and three older brothers. She would have been the thirteenth child but, by 1878, eight babies had already died very young.[1]

Victor Castel, six years older than his wife, was a teacher in the public schools. Although the law had secularized all

---

[1] See VT 72, p. 296. Married at the age of fifteen, Mme. Castel brought nineteen children into the world in twenty-six years. Nine died at an early age. Gabrielle (1862-1938) entered the Providence Order in Lisieux. Michaëlle (1866-1927) and Violette (1879-1961) were care-takers at *Les Buissonnets* for several years. François (1867-1941) became a Brother of the Christian Schools, and later a lay priest and chaplain of the pilgrimage to Lisieux. Joachim, as we will see later, knew Fr. Brottier very well. The last one, Marguerite-Marie (1883-1964), entered the Visitation Order in Caen.

1

schools in 1882, he continued to say morning prayers with his students every day. This intransigent attitude clearly displeased the administration, and rather quickly he was forced to resign.

Settling in Paris

M. Castel went with his family to Paris and settled as a merchant in the quarters of the *rue de Vangirard*. He also started to work for Fr. Roussel, who had founded in Paris the "Work for First Communion," a program that helped abandoned children in the capital to prepare for their First Holy Communion. Fr. Roussel used the talents of this venerable teacher by sending him all around France to give conferences — especially to the seminaries — to make known and promote his Work

Thus Marie-Louise became a "little Parisian." For four years she went to school at the Daughters of the Cross in the *rue de l'abbé Groult*. When she was ten-and-a-half, she made her First Communion at the parish of St. Lambert. On that same day, May 21, 1885, Thérèse Martin renewed hers in the boarding school of the abbey in Lisieux. That afternoon, Marie-Louise received the sacrament of Confirmation.

An atmosphere of prayer

The family loved to pray to the Virgin before an image of Our Lady of Perpetual Help, the only well-known icon among French Catholics at that time; coming from Rome, this devotion had spread after 1866, under the impetus of the Redemptorist Fathers. In this image one sees Mary in the process of calming the Child Jesus, who is frightened by the vision of the "instruments of the Passion" that two angels are presenting to him.

But Marie-Louise's parents were inflamed most of all by a great devotion to the Holy Face. Following the example of a M. Dupont, a layman of Touraine who had contributed greatly to the revival of this devotion to the Holy Face several years earlier, M. Castel had transformed one of the rooms of his house into an oratory, where he had a little lamp burning night and day before the holy image. It is not astonishing that in such a family atmosphere, Marie-Louise readily turned to the Lord, and that at an early age she heard a call to religious life resonating in her heart. But she did not know exactly what God expected of her.

Discovery of a vocation

When she was twelve years old, she discovered a prayer entitled *To ask for light on one's vocation*. Immediately she undertook to recite it nine days in a row. At the end of the novena, while she was praying in front of the image of the Holy Face, she felt enlightened: "How happy the Carmelites must be," she said to herself. "I will be a Carmelite!"

A year later, a very slight incident shook the whole family quite a lot. One day they found the lamp broken that burned in the oratory. To replace it, Marie-Louise offered a crystal glass that was precious to her. One morning when M. Castel came into the oratory, he noticed that the crystal was all black, with a little brown triangle imprinted on it. He tried to wipe it off but could not make it disappear. Keenly affected by this trinitarian "symbol," he called his children and asked them if they saw this as a wink — a sign — from the Lord. When he came to Marie, she cried out: "The Holy Face did this marvelous thing for me, because it's on *my* glass that this triangle has formed!" One day when she was alone at home, she cleaned the lamp with some sand to check it out: the beautiful triangle was well etched in the glass! Let's not smile too quickly at this naivete but, instead, respect the ways by which God reveals to each of his children their particular vocation. Later, Marie-Louise's faith had plenty of time to ripen and mature.

The desire for Carmel became stronger in the young girl's

heart. This didn't keep her from remaining very impulsive and from living a very happy life in the capital city. Often, without her parents knowing it, she frequented the shops, the shows and the markets. In a *jeu de massacre*,[2] she showed a somewhat mischievous pleasure in focusing on the figures of priests or religious. Not for reasons of anticlericalism, she later said, "but for devotion."[3]

Yet, within her innermost self, the desire for these distractions was surpassed by the ever-increasing desire to love and to be loved. The Lord made her feel even then that only He could fill the infinite gap of nothingness in her heart. Sr. Thérèse of the Child Jesus later expressed this same desire, in a poem from May 1897, in which she delighted to sing about the loving mercy with which the Lord watches over his spouse who is like "a lily among thorns":

> *When my young heart caught fire with this flame*
> *That is called love, you came to claim it…*
> *And you alone, O Jesus, can satisfy my soul*
> *Which needs to love without measure or end.*[4]

Marie-Louise could no longer wait for the moment to consecrate herself to God by entering Carmel. Fr. Charles, chaplain of St. Geneviève d'Asnières, her boarding school, permitted her to make a private vow of virginity — a permission which he

---

[2] These were performances at town and country fairs where ecclesiastical, social and political authorities were portrayed by the common people who could thus give voice to their own perceptions of how they experienced these different authorities. It was forbidden to do this in the course of daily life; the context of the fair was the only acceptable way for people to publicly display their negative emotions against the ruling authorities with impunity. In this case, the *jeu de massacre* was possibly a performance about the French Revolution with its massacres, in which the clergy were portrayed in a somewhat negative manner. Authorities were sometimes represented as wooden objects depicting different persons and events from life and history. These plays are still a popular public spectacle in our own day at European fairs on feast days (trans.).

[3] Obituary, p. 3.

[4] PN 53, 2.

granted also to one of her classmates who likewise desired to enter Carmel. During a noon break for lunch, the two girls sneaked off to the school chapel to pronounce their vows. It was the day in May 1890, when the school children came to make their First Communion. The chapel was completely filled with flowers and the great Gospel Book was open in the choir for the renewal of baptismal promises which were to be made in the afternoon. With their hand placed on the Gospel, each of the two young girls promised the Lord to belong to no one but himself. In three months, Marie-Louise would be sixteen.

First contacts with Carmel

Some weeks later, Marie-Louise learned from her confessor that the prioress of the Carmel at *l'avenue de Messine* had accepted her for an eight-day retreat in the monastery guest house. The superior asked only that she write to her, giving the reasons why she was interested in entering Carmel. Marie-Louise remembered having read a list of twelve reasons in her classmate's notebook. "If I present all twelve," the teenager said to herself, "Mother Prioress will certainly find one that is valuable!" She took it upon herself to write a long letter that began: "Reverend Mother, you have asked me the reasons why I desire to enter Carmel. To be honest, I know only one: God calls me and I come. He has suffered even to die out of love for me; I want to suffer out of love for him. But here are twelve reasons why I want to leave the world."[5] And Marie-Louise enumerated the twelve motives found in her friend's notebook.

During her vacation at Pentecost she went to the parlor of Carmel to meet the prioress, who assured her that she was in no way touched by her long list of reasons. "On the contrary," she added, "it was only the beginning of your letter that assured

---

[5] *Story of My Vocation*, VT 72, p. 298.

me of your vocation." Marie-Louise did not dare to reveal the source of her text, but was thrilled to know that only her personal reasons had influenced the prioress' decision.

When the school year ended, she went to the monastery as planned, to again participate in the spiritual exercises. She met with the extraordinary confessor of the Carmelites, Fr. Blino, S.J., who had returned from giving a retreat at the Carmel in Lisieux. In the course of their meeting, Fr. Blino spoke to Marie-Louise about a certain Sr. Thérèse of the Child Jesus who, before entering the monastery, had gone all the way to Rome in order to receive the pope's permission to enter Carmel at the age of fifteen. Obviously he was not telling Marie-Louise something that was confessional matter. When Thérèse had shared with him her desire to become a saint and to love God as much as Teresa of Avila, her patroness, he had responded to her rather shortly: "Sister, you would do better to correct your faults, make a little progress in virtue each day and temper your rash desires!"[6]

At the end of this retreat, Marie-Louise was intimately convinced of the seriousness of her Carmelite vocation, and wanted to start her postulancy right away. But the prioress judged it prudent to put off her entrance for eight months.

In the Carmel of l'avenue de Messine

So it was that on April 30, 1891, the young girl passed through the cloister door and received the name Sr. Agnes of Jesus. The postulant particularly loved this Carmel because it was specially dedicated to the prayer of making reparation to the humiliated Face of the Savior. There were numerous contacts between the Carmel in Paris and the one in Tours where Sr. Marie of St. Peter had received the mission of developing

---

[6] Mother Agnes of Jesus, NPPA, *Espérance*, p. 2.

this particular devotion of making reparation to the Holy Face. Very rapidly Sr. Agnes perceived that it isn't always easy to pray and that the joy of pleasing God in all circumstances doesn't eliminate the difficult character of certain mortifications. But fairly quickly, she also understood that this absence of "consolations" is not a sign of "no vocation." On May 12, 1892, one year after her entrance, she took the habit and began her novitiate. At the end of the year, Fr. Boulanger, provincial of the Order of Friars Preachers, gave a retreat from December 9-16, that impressed the young novice very much. We will see later the manner in which she talked about it to Sr. Thérèse of the Child Jesus. Unfortunately, the novice's health kept getting worse, so that she had to leave Carmel on July 8, 1893. Her father took her to Trouville in order that she regain her strength.

It was through the frequent news letters exchanged between the Carmels in Lisieux and in Paris that Sr. Thérèse of the Child Jesus learned during July that a very young novice had just left the monastery of *l'avenue de Messine*. And since there was now a legal plan under discussion, aimed at forbidding religious communities to receive candidates younger than 21, Thérèse said: "*If they were to send me away, I know very well what I would do: I would go find little Sr. Agnes of Jesus and we would live together until we had reached the age to re-enter Carmel!*"[7]

Towards the Carmel of Lisieux

Marie-Louise so profited from her sojourn on the Norman coast that on July 22, she went to the Carmel of Lisieux to seek there a little spiritual strength. She was welcomed by a Sister who bore her same name, Sr. Agnes of Jesus, Thérèse's real sister [Pauline], and who had become prioress on February 20, 1893. We remember that it was Pauline whom Thérèse had

---

[7] Germaine, 8/12/08.

spontaneously adopted as her "second mama" after the death of Mme. Martin in 1877 — and not her elder sister and god-mother Marie, who had also entered the Carmel of Lisieux under the name Sr. Marie of the Sacred Heart.

We recall that another sister of Thérèse, Céline, her insepa-rable companion in their childhood games, will enter this Carmel the following year [1894], after their father's death. She made her profession in February 1896, under the name Sr. Geneviève, and died in 1959, at the age of 90. As for Léonie, the third daughter of the Martin family, she went again to enter the Visitation order in Caen for a new attempt at religious life, but it was in January 1899 that she finally entered to stay. She made her profession in July 1900, under the name Sr. Frances-Thérèse, and died there in June 1941, at the age of 78.

But let us get back to the Carmel of Lisieux in July 1893. The convalescent Marie-Louise also met Mother Marie de Gonzague, the former prioress who, since February, was in charge of the novitiate. The fraternal welcome that Marie-Louise received at Lisieux encouraged her to return often during the summer months.

Back in Paris, Marie-Louise learned that the superior of the Carmel was opposed to her re-entering the community before she was 21, and that it was necessary for her to take time to com-pletely restore her health. Marie-Louise was distressed! The prioress of *l'avenue de Messine* suggested that she ask permis-sion to enter the Carmel of Lisieux, saying that the country air would do her more good than staying in Paris.

Mother Agnes of Jesus and Mother Marie de Gonzague ac-cepted her, but this time again, they had to overcome the reluc-tance of the famous Canon Delatroëtte, the superior of the Lisieux Carmel, the same one who, previously, was so fero-ciously opposed to the entrance of Thérèse. One day when Marie-Louise felt more discouraged than ever, she begged the Holy Virgin to soften the Canon's heart, so that she could enter Carmel on the feast of Our Lady of Perpetual Help. Her prayer was heard and she won her way, entering the cloister at the *rue de Livarot* in Lisieux on June 16, 1894 — but not without taking a last ride on the merry-go-round at the Lisieux fair!

Her parents no longer lived in Paris; M. and Mme. Castel had moved back to their native Normandy and established themselves with their children in Lisieux. Some days after the entry of Marie-Louise into Carmel, Marguerite-Marie, her little sister, the youngest of the family, made her First Communion at her Providence boarding school. In the afternoon she presented herself at the grille of Carmel to visit her big sister there. Thérèse, who accompanied the brand new novice to the parlor, could not help but think of what had happened in the same spot on May 8, 1884, the day of her own First Communion. Wearing her all-white Communion dress, she had come to admire her dear sister Pauline in the all-black long veil of a professed nun.

II. IN THE CARMEL OF LISIEUX (1894-1944)

A) AT THE TIME OF THÉRÈSE

Upon entering the Carmel of Lisieux, the novice received the name Sr. Marie-Agnes of the Holy Face. Mother Agnes of Jesus gave her Sr. Thérèse of the Child Jesus as an "angel." This was the name given to the nun in charge of initiating a novice into the customs of the monastery and the spirit of Carmel.

In fact, Thérèse herself was still "a novice." Although she had made her profession more than three years earlier — the time after which a professed officially leaves the novitiate — she had asked Mother Agnes on September 8, 1893, to stay there longer. It is true that having two sisters already in the chapter, she could not function according to her right [as a voting member], nor be named for an official position. Mother Agnes had willingly accepted Thérèse's request, seeing that this situation would permit her to more easily watch over the two novices who would be confided to her, Sr. Martha and Sr. Marie-Madeleine.

A great joy for Thérèse

Thérèse was delighted about the arrival of Sr. Marie-Agnes of the Holy Face in the novitiate. Finally, she was no longer the benjamin of the community; the new novice was her junior. And by a marvelous coincidence, this was the same young Sister of the *rue de Messine* who had had to leave Carmel just one year before.

She seemed so young, her round face still looked so much like a child's, that Thérèse later called her *"my little doll,"* an affectionate nickname that long ago she had given to her cousin Marie Guérin — a nickname that would well express how Thérèse, at the end of her own life, truly considered this novice as her daughter. But Thérèse never "mothered" her doll; on the contrary, she treated her rather severely, and did not allow her any whims.

There was another reason for joy: the newcomer had a strong, pleasing voice. Thérèse certainly noticed it on June 24, feast of St. John the Baptist, the day when the Carmelites "chanted" the Office — which at that time meant that they sang *recto tono* [monotone] on a higher pitch than usual! After the Office ended, Thérèse went to find the novice and said to her: *"I am so happy! I had asked God that I might have a daughter who would have a strong voice to support the choir, in order to supply what I can't give, and behold! He has granted me that desire! You have just the voice that I would wish to have. Now, I am no longer pained at not having one, since God has given me a daughter who has enough voice for both of us!"*[8]

We remember that Thérèse didn't sing particularly well and that in this month of June 1894, her voice started to sound hoarse. Her throat was sore and she had a cough. On June 18, two days after Marie-Louise's entrance into Carmel, her throat began to be treated: *"Two days after the entrance of Sr. Marie of*

---

[8] CSM 32.

the Trinity, my throat was treated," Thérèse would later recall. *"God has permitted the novices to exhaust me. Sr. Marie of the Eucharist* [Marie Guérin] *told me that this is happening to me like it does to all preachers."*[9]

In fact, a wonderful friendship was going to be born between the two Carmelites that would allow Thérèse to communicate her spiritual discoveries to a heart perfectly prepared to receive them. Together with Céline, who in her turn entered the novitiate on September 14 of this same year, Sr. Marie-Agnes of the Holy Face was going to become a privileged witness of the "Little Way" that Thérèse would discover at the end of this year, 1894. It is even probable that Thérèse's new responsibility towards the novices obliged her in some way to better refine what she will later call her "little doctrine."

As for Marie-Louise, she saw that a wish of hers was coming true, the one that she had confided with great simplicity one day to her novice mistress in Paris: to be inspired in her efforts by the presence at her side of a companion who would be a guide and a friend at the same time.

A difficult novice

Thérèse had a hard job to help her youngest novice. Her unsuccessful attempt in another Carmel didn't win her the good graces of the Lisieux community, and her very lively demeanor as a "little Parisian" didn't make her seem "very serious." The postulant had little aptitude for that modesty of look and gesture that is considered one of the distinctive marks of a Carmelite. To be convinced of this, it suffices to read one of the first paragraphs of the Book of Decorum which served as the basis of the novices' formation, "Concerning modesty and mortification of the senses":

---

[9] CJ 7.29.6.

— "The Sisters must take great care to manage and com-
pose their exterior appearance the best they can, in order
to honor that of Our Lord Jesus Christ and of his most
blessed Mother."

— "They must always hold themselves erect and, whether
speaking or walking, they must pay attention to make
the least movement possible of the head, the hands and
the rest of the body."

— "They must go about the house in a recollected and
extremely modest manner, without turning the head,
nor raising their gaze to look at anything out of curiosity
or frivolity, and they must keep their hands under the
scapular so that they will refrain from carrying anything
that would hinder them."

— "They must pay attention to train their feet to make so
little noise while walking, that they will not be heard at
all. Our Spanish Mothers were very exact in this practice, and they strongly urged it."[10]

For a long time this had been told to the novice mistresses,
that the first quality of a Carmelite was "exterior comportment."

And other paragraphs of the work — which the novice
mistress commented upon at the novitiate meetings — included
these similar recommendations:

— "When someone truly needs to speak, if two words will
suffice, one must render this accuracy to God and not
say three."[11]

— "During the Hours of the Office, one must be most
modest and recollected, and pay great attention to not
raise the eyes at all, and not turn the head at all, nor
touch one's face or one's clothing."[12]

---

[10] *Le Papier d'exaction apporté en France par nos Mères espagnoles*, Paris, J. Mersch,
1889, p. 7.

[11] *Ibid.*, p. 3.

[12] *Ibid.*, p. 14.

Carmelites are asked to keep this mastery of gesture and glance in the refectory as well:

— "They ought always to have their eyes cast down and fixed before them, without turning the head, and without looking at others, even when serving them. [...] They ought always to hold themselves erect, leaning neither on the table nor against the wall."[13]

Despite the two years that she had already spent in Carmel, the novice retained a certain difficulty in yielding to this rule. Far from keeping her eyes down in her travels, she loved to look about inquisitively everywhere, which obliged Thérèse to comment to her that her glances resembled too much those of a *"wild rabbit."*[14]

Thérèse understood better than the novice herself, how in one's youth one likes to actively move around. It sufficed to remember that her own preferred games were the see-saw and jump-rope. But her concern to refuse Our Lord nothing, her desire also to use all the humble little means that favored continual prayer, had made her succeed to an extraordinary degree in self-mastery. Mother Agnes loved to recall that her little sister "seemed to proceed slowly,"[15] yet always finished her work on schedule. By never hastening her step, Thérèse likewise irritated the very nuns who were noticeably most active in the community, like Sr. Marie-Philomène. For the same reason, Sr. Saint-Stanislaus had nicknamed Thérèse "Sr. Amen,"[16] and Sr. St. Vincent de Paul called her "the big nanny goat."

It was also known that the gardener would recognize the silhouette of Sr. Thérèse of the Child Jesus under her veil, by

---

[13] *Ibid.*, p. 23.

[14] LT 167.

[15] Postscript to a letter from Marie of the Trinity to Sr. Germaine, 7/17/09.

[16] Because she came at the end, like the Amen at the end of a prayer (trans.).

the way she walked with great recollection. Thérèse hoped for a similar evolution in the novice's carriage and above all in her interior disposition.

Taking of the Habit

In other respects, Sr. Marie-Agnes' progress was sufficient so that she was authorized to again receive the habit of Carmel on December 18, 1894, the feast of the Expectation [pregnancy] of the Virgin. Thérèse composed two poems for this occasion. The first one, entitled *"Finally the time of tears is over,"* allowed the new novice to sing her gratitude to the Holy Virgin, while also addressing a discreet thank you to the Sisters of the community. At the same time, Thérèse showed Sr. Marie-Agnes of the Holy Face that an entire program of spiritual life is found inscribed in her religious name: to live hidden under Mary's mantle and in the light of the Holy Face:

> *Your Son's indescribable gaze* [le regard]
> *has deigned to lower itself upon my poor soul.*
> *I have been searching for his adorable Face*
> *and it is in him that I wish to hide myself.*
> *I must always remain small*
> *to merit the attention* [les regards] *of his eyes.*[17]

The second poem was likewise addressed to the Virgin. Sung by the choir of Carmelites, its purpose was to welcome the novice into her new community. With an exquisite delicacy, Thérèse gave a biblical coloring to this *second* investiture:

> *The rough serge is finally returned;*
> *Twice she has taken your habit.*
> *O, that she may also be clothed anew,*
> *Mother, with a double portion of your spirit!*[18]

---

[17] PN 11, 3.
[18] PN 12, 4.

It isn't impossible that this allusion to the mantle of Elijah, conferring upon his disciple Elisha a double portion of his spirit [cf. 2 Kings 2:9ff.], had occurred to Thérèse by the fact that she lived in the cell named St. Elisha during the month of August 1894.

Spiritual accompaniment

Under her brand new habit, Sr. Marie-Agnes was far from being perfect and nobody missed an opportunity to let her know it! One day, when she was severely reprimanded, she went, very discouraged, to look for Thérèse and said to her: "I don't have a vocation any more!" As an answer she received only a laugh from her elder. Since then, Marie-Agnes said later, "Whenever something didn't work out and I went to find her, she forestalled my complaints by saying, 'So, you don't have a vocation anymore?'[19] That de-dramatized the problem, for sure!"

Thérèse did not spare her novice pain in order to help her progress, but she also pleaded her cause before the Sisters in the community who had more difficulty in handling her impetuous temperament. *"How, with all my heart, I would give my life for you to be a Carmelite!"*[20] Thérèse said to her often.

Sr. Marie-Agnes experienced a real veneration for Thérèse. Witness this tiny little incident which the former novice mentioned in the apostolic Process: "I wasn't happy that she didn't want to receive me, and I wanted her to feel my bad mood by not talking to her the whole day. In the evening she came to find me and as I was preparing to reproach her, I was suddenly seized by a supernatural feeling when I looked at her, that completely changed my dispositions.

"Ever since then," she continued, "I could no longer keep myself from a certain respect mingled with admiration for her,

---

[19] CSM 37.
[20] CRM 43.

that grew greater every day."[21] An admiration that, far from hindering trust, favored it. People could tell Thérèse everything, even the criticisms that they desired to "make" to her or that they had a mind to "report" to her. Sr. Marie-Agnes experienced more than once the truth of what Thérèse wrote in her last manuscript: *"I prefer vinegar to sugar; also my soul gets tired of food that is too sweet and Jesus permits someone to serve him a good little salad, well seasoned with vinegar and spices; nothing is missing except the oil. This good little salad is being served to me by the novices at a time when I least expect it. [...] With a simplicity that delights me, they tell me about all the struggles I give them and what about me displeases them; finally, they are under no restraint anymore than if they were talking about someone else, knowing that they give me great pleasure to act like this."*[22]

"Knowing the true pleasure I was causing her," said the novice later, "I didn't hide one of the bitter words that I was able to hear (about her or about her sisters)."[23]

Thérèse was striving to form the novice in genuine humility. She told her one day: *"A very abundant and choice meal will be served in your honor. Fortunately for you, I will pass by at that moment and, like a mother for her child, I will eagerly collect these substantial foods. I will bring them to you because I think that they will do you good and please you as much as they do me."* These foods were obviously the criticisms that Thérèse kept hearing on the subject of Sr. Marie-Agnes.

"Promise me," she said when she ended this conversation, *"that you will act for me as I act for you. Look how I give you proofs of a true love; since you love me, give me these same proofs."*[24]

---

[21] CRM 89.
[22] C 27 r.
[23] CRM 78.
[24] CRM 79.

Family concerns

Thérèse didn't understand the saints who didn't love their families. No wonder that she often encouraged Sr. Marie-Agnes to tell her about her brothers and sisters still living — four were older, four were younger. Thérèse said to her: *"Entrust them to God and don't worry about them any further; everything will turn out well for them. If you worry about them yourself, God won't worry about them and you will deprive your parents of the graces that you would have obtained for them by leaving it to him."*[25]

This abandonment produced wonders. The novice could experience this more perceptibly in 1895, it seemed to her, regarding something that happened in the middle of Lent. One morning she went to tell Thérèse the dream that she had just had: finding herself near her sister Anna, she began to explain to her Thérèse's poem *To Live by Love*, to urge her to consecrate herself to the Lord. "Must I not write to my sister," continued the novice, "to tell her about my dream and to share with her my presentiments about her vocation?"

But it was not the custom of Carmel to send out mail during Lent. Consulted on this matter, Mother Marie de Gonzague judged that there was no reason to make an exception to the rule; it is by prayer that Carmelites must enlighten and save souls.

The two of them then began to pray with all their heart: *"What joy,"* they said to themselves, *"if it would be granted to us at the end of Lent!" "Oh! infinite mercy of the Lord, who really wants to answer the prayers of his little children. [...] At the end of Lent,"* recounted Thérèse in her last manuscript, *"one more soul consecrated herself to Jesus. It was a true miracle of grace, a miracle obtained by the ardor of a humble novice!"*[26]

Sr. Marie-Agnes also told Thérèse about the help that her father gave to the Work founded by Fr. Roussel. She didn't sus-

---

[25] CRM 22-23.
[26] C 25 r.

pect that Thérèse would become, a quarter of a century later, the heavenly collaborator of Fr. Brottier who revived this wonderful Work in 1923 and gave it the scope that it later had.

The Holy Face

The young mistress and her novice both had a great devotion to the Holy Face. They also had it at heart to help each other live in his light.

Thanks to Sr. Marie-Agnes of the Holy Face, the Lisieux Carmel adopted a paraliturgical custom which had been practiced for many years at the Paris Carmel. On Monday of Holy Week, a large engraving of the Holy Face was exposed in the oratory, and after the Gospel reading recounting the anointing at Bethany [Jn 12:1-9], every nun went to anoint the forehead and feet of the Savior with a piece of cotton impregnated with perfume.

On her part, Sr. Thérèse of the Child Jesus and of the Holy Face loved to share with her novice what she had discovered from having pondered Veronica's Veil for a long time. On August 6, 1895, in solemnly celebrating the feast of the Lord's Transfiguration, the Carmelites, following the custom of the brethren at Tours, honored his adorable and disregarded Face. Several days later, on August 12, Sr. Marie-Agnes received as a present for her twenty-first birthday a poem by Thérèse. In it Thérèse reminded her of the importance of the Holy Countenance in a contemplative life. This contemplation is a foretaste of the joy of heaven, from which comes the title of the poem, *My heaven here below.*

> *"Jesus, your ineffable image*
> *is the star guiding my steps.*
> *Ah! you know that your sweet countenance*
> *is, for me, heaven here below."*

This contemplative regard creates a desire to resemble what it beholds. Whereas in the Paris Carmel, as also in Tours, the veneration of the Holy Face was motivated principally by the desire to make reparation for the outrages committed "against the majesty of God, the divinity of our Lord and the authority of the Church," Thérèse insisted almost exclusively on the necessity of resemblance to the humiliated Face of Jesus. It is, moreover, by hiding in it that one ends up resembling him:

> *"Your Face is my only wealth:*
> *I ask for nothing more.*
> *In it, hiding myself unceasingly,*
> *I will resemble you, Jesus."*

And finally, in regarding Jesus this way, one draws souls towards him and prepares oneself for the final encounter with him:

> *"That I may gather*
> *A beautiful golden harvest,*
> *Set me ablaze with your flames!*
> *With your adorable mouth*
> *give me soon the eternal kiss!..."*[27]

Offering to Merciful Love

Having entered the novitiate on December 18, 1894, Sr. Marie-Agnes of the Holy Face could make her profession at the end of 1895. But Mother Marie de Gonzague, the official mistress of novices, believed that she was not yet ready to pronounce her perpetual vows. Besides, she perhaps wanted to reserve the "honor" of receiving this commitment when she would be — at least, she hoped to be — the prioress again. Be

---

[27] PN 20.

that as it may, the profession was postponed until April 30, 1896. Thérèse suggested to the novice not to wait for this date to surrender herself entirely to Love. On November 30, Thérèse proposed to her to pronounce, the very next morning, her Act of Oblation to the Merciful Love of God. It is thus that on December 1, 1895, the first Sunday of Advent, Sr. Marie-Agnes, kneeling close to Thérèse in the community chapel, prolonged her thanksgiving before the Blessed Sacrament exposed, and pronounced there her Act of Oblation. This very day, she later confided, "I was so flooded with graces... that all day long I experienced in a very tangible way the presence of the Eucharistic Jesus in my heart."[28]

Sr. Marie of the Trinity and of the Holy Face

1896. The hour of profession approached. Two months earlier, on Friday, March 6 — the day of Lent when the feast of the Holy Shroud was celebrated [Friday of the second week of Lent] — it was decided that Sr. Marie-Agnes of the Holy Face would henceforth be called Sr. Marie of the Trinity and of the Holy Face. Why this change? Quite simply, because the local dialect made little distinction between "*Marie*-Agnes" and "*Mère* [Mother] Agnes" (which a Norman tends to pronounce like "*Mâre* Agnes"). In order to avoid every risk of confusion between the names of the two Carmelites, it was better to give Sr. Marie-Agnes a different name, the one that for a moment had been considered for Thérèse's sister Céline.

Several weeks later, the future professed understood in a flash how much the new name suited her perfectly. Hardly had she been officially presented to the chapter regarding her profession, than she felt fear. During Compline she suddenly imagined that she had taken the wrong path and that she should have

---

[28] CSM 39. See pp. 69-70.

understood more quickly, from the numerous difficulties encountered in the two Carmels of Paris and Lisieux, that she did not at all have a Carmelite vocation. But instantly she remembered the brown triangle burnt into the glass that she had offered to the Holy Face years ago. "Sr. Marie of the Trinity and of the Holy Face" couldn't help seeing this sudden reminder of her childhood as a response from heaven to her scruples. In her heart peace expelled anxiety.

The next day she went to share her joy with Thérèse who, very moved herself, easily revealed the meaning of the allegory: *"The glass that first became all black,"* she told her, *"is the image of your soul during that night of your long trials; one could not yet recognize God's designs upon you. Slowly everything cleared up, becoming transparent again, and one discovers that the Holy Trinity had always marked you with His divine seal. Your end will also resemble that of this same glass which broke under the heat of too strong a flame: the ardent flame of divine Love will break your mortal shell. Ah! Spend your life in gratitude, because you are particularly loved by God!"*[29]

The profession

On April 30, 1896, five years to the day of her first entrance into the Paris Carmel, Sr. Marie of the Trinity finally pronounced her vows. "This day," she noted in her diary, "became more of heaven than of earth… Sr. Thérèse of the Child Jesus seemed as happy as I was. *'I look like Joan of Arc assisting at the coronation of Charles VII,'* she said to me."[30] This humble pride of Thérèse is reflected in the way she looks in the photograph taken that day. "Between the child and the elderly woman, between the kneeling novice with a mischievous smile and the seated prioress marked by the 'irreparable ravages of age,' Thérèse holds

---

[29] Obituary, p. 7.
[30] *Story of My Vocation*, p. 302.

herself erect, like a mild and strong mediator, serene and serious."[31]

For this occasion, Thérèse wrote still two more poems. The first, intended to be sung at chapter, contained a discrete allusion to the Offering that the newly professed had already made of herself on December 1, 1895.[32]

The second one, written in calligraphy on the back of an image of the Holy Face, recaptured a poem of John of the Cross that Thérèse specially loved: *Thoughts on the Divine*. In giving her this image, Thérèse made the young professed pay attention to the thought that she loved the most: *"Love knows how to draw profit from everything: from the good and from the bad that is found in us."*[33] Such is, in fact, the conviction that dwelt more and more in Thérèse's soul and which is at the heart of her "Little Way": in order to be purified from our faults of frailty that we have the misfortune to commit, we need to be re-immersed unceasingly in the consuming Fire of love. Thérèse thus reminded Marie of the Trinity that she must never let herself be discouraged.

Several months later Thérèse wrote: *"I am only a feeble and powerless child: nevertheless it is my weakness itself that gives me the audacity to offer myself as a victim to your Love, O Jesus [...]. Yes, that Love be completely satisfied, It must abase Itself, lower Itself to nothingness so that It can transform this nothingness into fire."*[34]

What Marie of the Trinity didn't realize was the spiritual night in which her novice mistress had found herself for the past month, which gave a unique highlight to the thoughts of John of the Cross that she recaptured in the poem:

> *"Supported without any support,*
> *Without Light and in Darkness*

---

[31] *Poems*, vol. I, p. 158.

[32] PN 29, 11.

[33] PN 30 — CSM 31.

[34] B 3 v.

I walk, consumed by Love…
On the way that I must follow
To encounter more than one danger,
But by love I will live well
in the Darkness of exile."[35]

That evening, the newly professed found her bed covered with forget-me-nots and a note that Thérèse had put there:

"My darling little sister,

I would like to have immortal flowers[36] *to offer you, in remembrance of this beautiful day, but it is only in heaven that flowers won't ever wilt!…*

These forget-me-nots will at least tell you that in the heart of your little sister there will always be engraved the remembrance of the day when Jesus gave you his Kiss of union."[37]

One week later, on the occasion of the taking of the veil, there was a new gift from Thérèse. On the back of an image of John of the Cross, she had copied three of the saint's texts; in particular, the ones where the Spanish doctor affirms: "When the love that one gives to a creature is a completely spiritual affection and founded on God alone, then in the measure that we believe in this affection, in the same measure God's love also believes in our soul. The more the heart remembers the beloved, the more it also remembers God and desires that these two loves

---

[35] PN 30.

[36] *Fleurs immortelles* are what we call "dry flowers," but Thérèse was making a play on words (trans.).

[37] Thérèse also offered to the young professed an image representing the Presentation of Mary in the Temple, which she commented upon thus, in giving it to her: *"You are the little Mary who climbs the steps of the Temple. To the left of the high priest, I am the child who calls you by making a sign with the hand; Céline sits on his* [the high priest's] *shoulder; and there, on the other side, is Sr. Marie of the Eucharist* [Marie Guérin]." It was the same image of the Presentation that Thérèse had received from Sr. Agnes [Pauline] the day of her profession, September 8, 1890 (CSM 42).

might grow and increase, vying to imitate each other."[38] A discreet way for Thérèse to explain to her novice that she shouldn't have any scruples about feeling the profound spiritual affection that was developing between them. It was a very pure friendship that helped both of them draw nearer to God.

Novitiate meetings

On March 21, 1896, after a troublesome election process, Mother Marie de Gonzague again became the prioress of the community. Thérèse was invested with an official authority over the novices. She refused to exercise the office of novice mistress — a position which she left to her prioress — but accepted the delicate role of being her assistant for the five novices then in the novitiate.

The job was difficult. Four of them were older than Thérèse and not always willing to take her smiling but firm direction. One found her severe. Sr. Marie-Madeleine remained "blocked." And it happened that the prioress, always jealous for her authority, contradicted the decisions of the young sister in charge, who remained until her death a simple novice among the novices. Considering this situation, one can better understand the prayer that she made at the moment of accepting her task:

> *Lord, I am too small to nourish your children; if you want to give them through me what each one needs, fill my little hand and without leaving your arms, without turning my head, I will give your treasures to the soul that comes to me asking for her nourishment. If she finds it to her taste, I will know that she doesn't owe it to me but to you. On the contrary, if she complains and finds what I offer her bitter, my peace shall not be troubled. I will try to convince her that this nourishment comes from you and I will restrain myself from seeking something else for her.*[39]

---

[38] LT 188.
[39] C 22 r-v.

Every day at 2:30 p.m., Thérèse met with the novices for half an hour to explain the Rule and the customs, to correct faults and to answer questions that a novice can have at the beginning of her life of prayer: "What do you do when your mind is invaded by distractions?" asked Marie of the Trinity. Thérèse answered: *"I also have a lot of these, but as soon as I perceive them I pray for the persons that occupy my imagination and this way they benefit from my distractions."*[40]

The mistress of the novitiate chiefly taught the "Little Way" that she had discovered by reading Scripture and that she valued more and more for its magnificent effectiveness: the road of confidence to reach Love. She thought out parables to make herself better understood, trying to adapt herself to each novice. We will see in the course of this work that Marie of the Trinity gathered these lessons with care and she lived them.

Small means in the service of love

Thérèse also invented tiny ways to get to the very root of certain faults in her novice. Marie of the Trinity still cried very easily. Despite the title given to the poem Thérèse wrote for Marie's investiture in December 1894, "The time of tears" was not yet "over"! But how could Thérèse be strict about it? Hadn't she herself suffered from this weakness for many years? It required a true psychological miracle for her to be freed of it once and for all, which had happened on Christmas night in 1886. But while waiting for a like miracle in the novice's character, Thérèse could at least help her to fight her whimperings.

One day Thérèse used a very simple method: "Taking from her painting table a mussel shell, and holding my hands to keep me from wiping my eyes, she caught my tears in this shell; my tears soon changed into a joyful smile." *"From now on"* —

---

[40] CRM 51.

Thérèse concluded — *"I allow you to cry as much as you want, but it must be into this shell."*[41] This episode must have taken place in 1896-1897, at a time when Thérèse worked officially as an "employed painter," doing remunerated work. After the death of Marie of the Trinity, the famous shell was found in her writing desk... along with a spinning-top. We are going to see why.

To encourage herself to practice virtue, the novice imagined herself playing ninepins [a game of bowling] with the Child Jesus. "The ninepins represent souls; they come in all sizes and in all colors in order to represent the ones that I would like to 'hit' in my prayer: little children, great fishermen, priests, religious, etc. The bowling ball is my love." When it seemed too difficult to win, the novice asked Jesus to play in her place.[42]

Obliged to verify that the novice was indeed making progress by following this childlike method, Thérèse encouraged her to pursue her "game." As she explained in her last manuscript: *"One realizes that it is absolutely necessary to forget one's tastes, one's personal conceptions and to guide souls on the way that Jesus has marked out for them, without trying to make them walk according to one's own way."*[43]

Another time, in December 1896, the novices received different nick-knacks for the Christmas tree. At the bottom of the package they found a strange object they couldn't identify. "It's a *top*," Marie of the Trinity exclaimed. "It's a lot of fun, it can spin all day long without stopping as long as you keep whipping it." And she gave them a demonstration then and there under the attentive glance of the novice mistress.

After Midnight Mass, the novice found the top in her cell with a letter from her "little Brother Jesus." He loves the ninepins but would like to change to another game and asks her to be his top. *"But strokes of the whip are necessary to make the top spin.*

---

[41] CSM 10.
[42] CSM 2.
[43] C 22 v - 23 r.

[...] Fine! let your[44] *Sisters render you this service and be thankful to those who will be most assiduous in not letting you slow down your spin. When I have been well entertained by you, I will bring you up above and we can play without any suffering."*[45]

It was important to make available to Marie of the Trinity, in one way or another, the teaching that John of the Cross had given in his day to the Carmelite nuns of Béas, which was later distributed to all the Carmelites:

> The first precaution in order to break away from all the troubles and all the imperfections that one encounters in the common life and in your relationships among the nuns, and also to draw profit from everything that happens is this: you must be utterly convinced that you have come to religious life only to be exercised and shaped by all your brothers and sisters. Know for certain that all who are in the convent — and this is perfectly true — are workmen charged with the task of forming you to perfection — some by word, others by deed, other by judgments they make against you. As for you: remain always submissive to events like a statue in the hands of the sculptor, the painter and the decorator. If you are not willing to do this, you will never live in harmony with the religious who surround you, nor will you gain holy peace or avoid a multitude of evils.[46]

Even to the end, Thérèse did not hesitate to employ child-like language to encourage her student to "grow in love." Witness this final note that Thérèse sent to her for her feastday on June 13, 1897, the feast of the Holy Trinity: *"May the divine little Jesus find in your soul a dwelling entirely perfumed with roses of Love;*

---

[44] Jesus speaks to her using the personal form of "you" (*tu*) and "your" (*toi*) (trans.).

[45] LT 212.

[46] *Spiritual Instructions and Precautions*, in *Spiritual Life and Work*, Poitiers, 1877, vol. I, pp. 372-373.

may he find there still the burning lamp of fraternal charity which will warm his cold little members."[47]

All of her life, moreover, Marie of the Trinity retained the language and demeanor of a child, even when she reached her full spiritual maturity and when she was gravely ill.

A great theologian

These childlike games didn't prevent her from being an open spirit interested in many things and also bringing Thérèse some very precious information. The former novice from Paris remembered, for example, the very intense conferences that were given in her Carmel in December 1892, by Fr. Boulanger, provincial of the Dominicans.

Perhaps she had partially taken notes in shorthand. We know only that she later recopied them in their entirety in a notebook of 315 pages. Be that as it may, for the feast of St. Martha on July 29, 1894, the community drew by lots certain phrases taken from the retreat of 1892. Thérèse was delighted to draw a passage inviting her to do everything out of love. And we know from what follows that Marie of the Trinity was very happy to show her mistress that she noticed similarities between the "Little Way" and the doctrine of the Dominican theologian. *"What consolation you give me"* — said Thérèse — *"you can't imagine! For me to know that my thinking is supported by an expert, a renowned theologian, gives me an incomparable joy."* And she asked Marie of the Trinity to tell her again everything she remembered *"from those teachings of this holy religious."*[48]

We can easily guess the expressions of the lecturer that found a favorable echo in Thérèse's heart, whether it was the novice's notes or her memory that could recall them after all those years:

---

[47] LT 246.
[48] CSM 46.

See how God is good: with a little bit of love, one gets through to him and his justice, his mercy. But when love is perfect, there will be no more judgment, no more court of law, nothing but a Father who waits for his children, who wants to take them in his arms and press them to his heart.

What then is perfect charity? I hear a young Sister telling me: "Father, am I following you? Can I hope to have perfect charity?" It is necessary that this word *perfect charity* doesn't overwhelm you; one doesn't speak in a manner to discourage you, as if it were something unattainable. When God has attached to perfect charity such great advantages, would he make it inaccessible? — No, it isn't! — The perfect charity that God asks of us isn't what befits God or the Virgin; it's what befits everyone.

An example will serve to help you understand the influence that God exercises on his little creatures. Put on a paper this little nothing that we call a zero. What is a zero? Absolutely nothing. What is more pitiful than a zero left all alone? But if you put the number 1 in front of your zero, it is penetrated by the life-giving power of this 1 and it is worth 10, 100, 1000. This simple 1 will make you comprehend His power [...].

We can say the same thing about Carmel. Take all the different parts of the monastery, one after another: the choir, the dormitory, the cells, the refectory. How small they are, how common! There is nothing, absolutely nothing but zeros! Put a Carmelite all alone in the middle of those zeros: all you have done is add another zero. It isn't she who brings everything to life. She will vainly go around in circles, she will find nothing there and she won't even be happy there, because the whole of Carmel isn't enough for her. But if at the head of all these zeros that make up the ensemble of your life, you place this grand and infinite One that we call God, all the rest will be penetrated by His presence, the world will no longer be for you what it was before: it will be the new heaven and the new earth [cf. Rv 21:1].

Thérèse recaptured this parable in her letter to Fr. Rouland on May 9, 1897: *"Let us work together for the salvation of souls. I can do very little, in fact absolutely nothing, if I were alone; what consoles me is to think that at your side I can be useful for something. In fact, zero by itself has no value, but when placed next to a 1, it becomes powerful, provided however that it be placed on the good side: after it and not before! ... That is where Jesus has placed me, and I hope to remain there always, following you from afar by prayer and sacrifice."*[49]

The atmosphere of the novitiate

We have already seen the prayer, full of confidence, which Thérèse had made when she was given responsibility for the novitiate, but there was nothing passive about her attitude. The novice mistress wasn't "doing nothing."

She wrote poems and short plays to teach her "little doctrine." In 1894, she studied in detail the major work by Henri Wallon about Joan of Arc to prepare her second play about the Maid of Orléans. Her new responsibility didn't diminish her literary activity. In spite of the tuberculosis that affected her whole organism more and more, Thérèse continued to "produce": between April 1896 and May 1897, she composed twenty-six poems and two little plays, which were called in the beatification Process "pious recreations."

In fact the rehearsals of these plays were genuine recreation for the novitiate. When in *The Flight to Egypt* Thérèse put the highway bandits Abramin, Izarn and Torcol on stage, there was no doubt that the novices truly enjoyed certain of their dramatic speeches. And when in *The Triumph of Humility*, they played the role of the devils, they made a "hellish clatter" during the rehearsals!

---

[49] LT 226.

In short, there was a lot going on in the novitiate. Besides, Mother Marie de Gonzague loved it: the old dowager was lively and happy! Thérèse's presence and her remarks did not engender melancholy. Like Francis de Sales, she believed that "a saint sad is a sad saint!" — a saying that she knew from her childhood, because she had copied it again and again over a whole page of writing paper. She did not like saints who were known to be always serious, "even at recreation"; she much preferred Théophane Vénard, whose constant cheerfulness she especially admired.

Thérèse possessed the true gifts of a comedienne; she mimicked wonderfully well the thousand oddities of her entourage, their ways of walking or expressing themselves. She didn't use her talent to hurt. We recall, rather, what had already been said about her in 1893 by Sr. Marie of the Angels, her former novice mistress: "A mystic, a comedienne, she was everything. She knew how to make you weep with devotion and just as easily make you burst with laughter at recreation."[50]

Be always happy

Marie of the Trinity was especially sensitive to the message of evangelical joy that emanated from Thérèse's whole being, a joy that was the fruit of her love. Thérèse sang about this love, for example, in a poem that she offered as a feastday gift to her novice on May 31, 1896, feast of the Holy Trinity.

For two months now, Thérèse knew that her death was near and night had fallen on her soul. Henceforth she had only one desire:

> *"I want to hide myself on earth,*
> *To be the last one in everything*
> *For you, Jesus! ...*

---

[50] CG II, p. 1176.

To please you is my only interest,
And my bliss is you, Jesus! ..."[51]

Mother Agnes later entitled this poem: *I am thirsty for Love.*
Judging by the numerous copies of rough drafts, this "thirst"
was cast in the form of poetry with difficulty this time. But
Thérèse was not looking to produce literary masterpieces. In
June of 1894, Marie of the Trinity gave her a book about how to
write poetry, that she had brought with her to Carmel. Thérèse
returned it quite quickly, saying: *"I prefer not to know all the rules:*
my poems are a spurt from the heart, an inspiration. I am in no way
interested in subjecting myself to organizing a work of the spirit into
an essay. At this price, I would rather renounce writing poetry."[52]

One can't thank the Lord enough to have brought together
Marie-Louise Castel and Sr. Thérèse of the Child Jesus. Without this friendship, we would be deprived of these poems in
which the greatest saint of modern times gave the best of her
heart to the "littlest" of her novices.

This friendship had to undergo a moment of hard testing.
In the autumn of 1896, there was a serious question of the possible departure of two novices to the Carmel of Saigon... and it
was precisely the two novices "preferred" by Thérèse: Sr.
Geneviève [Céline] and Sr. Marie of the Trinity. *"My heaven was*
full of clouds," Thérèse wrote later in recalling this trial; *"only the*
bottom of my heart remained calm and in peace."[53] The storm passed,
for the two novices remained in Lisieux where they could continue to benefit from the teachings of Thérèse. We in turn can
benefit from everything that their memory has conserved.

With much tact Thérèse made a special effort to show both
of them that they each had their special place in her heart. She
arranged, for example, for Marie of the Trinity to be near her in
a photograph from time to time: *"Today it's your turn; Sister*

---

[51] PN 31.
[52] CSM 34.
[53] C 9 v.

Geneviève is next to me in the family group photo, and you aren't there."[54]

A friendship becomes deeper

One can even say without risk of error that Marie of the Trinity benefited from an entirely privileged relationship with her novice mistress. She was, and indeed felt herself to be, "the daughter" of Thérèse. Thérèse did not need to put on "kid gloves" to talk to her as she sometimes had to do in addressing Sr. Geneviève, who was four years her senior. With Marie of the Trinity, Thérèse was totally "natural"; she could share the deepest thoughts with her, heart to heart, in a very simple style and in a jovial tone that suited perfectly the *message* that the one desired to transmit and the *character* that the other had no desire to give up. In short, a true "complicity" in the best sense of the word.

In the last month of their life together, their exchanges deepened even more. Thérèse went so far as to confide to her novice one day the temptations that assailed her on the subject of the hereafter. Marie of the Trinity was completely astonished: "But the luminous canticles that you're composing contradict what you're telling me!"

"*Ah!*" Thérèse responded, "*I sing what I want to believe, but it is without any feeling. I couldn't even tell you to what degree the night is dark in my soul, for fear that I would make you share my temptations…*"

"She only confided this to me," concluded the novice later, "so that I might never be in such doubt."[55]

Marie of the Trinity believed Thérèse to be a saint so much that one day she fell on her knees in front of her, joined her

---

[54] CRM 57.
[55] CRM 15.

hands together and cried out: "Oh, Sr. Thérèse of the Child Jesus, you aren't like the others! I am sure that after your death, people will prostrate before you saying, 'St. Thérèse of the Child Jesus, pray for us!'" Which earned her this amiable loving reprimand: *"You really are a baby! Come on, enough of making fun of me!"*[56] Although we know this episode only from what is said in the obituary of Marie of the Trinity, it fits well with her spontaneous character.

For her part, Thérèse didn't hesitate to confide to her novice the dreams she had on this subject of heaven. One day, for example, Thérèse told her: *"Last night I dreamed that you were asking me: 'When you are in heaven, where will you be placed?' Without hesitation, I answered you: 'On the knees of God and there I would keep talking into his ear!' Then you replied: 'And me, where will I be placed?' And I said to you: 'You, my little doll, you will be placed in my arms!'"* ... And Thérèse added: *"You must see how much I love you, since even in my dreams I think about you!"*

One day Thérèse even went so far as to say to her: *"I can't tell you that I love you more today than I did yesterday, because my love for you has become so intense that it cannot increase!"*[57]

More and more, Marie of the Trinity had the feeling that she was close to, that she was taking care of a "saint." Witness some of Thérèse's hair that she kept, since they cut each other's hair every two months, following the custom of Carmel at that time. It's true that people in that era were encouraged to keep similar relics. Didn't Thérèse herself have the happiness to receive on a handkerchief Mother Geneviève's last tear?[58] And hadn't she asked Fr. Roulland to send her a lock of his hair? *"For me, they will be relics,"* she had written him, *"when you will be in heaven with the martyr's palm in your hand."*[59]

In the spring of 1897, Thérèse's health took a dangerous

---

[56] Obituary, p. 14.
[57] CSM 52 and 51.
[58] A 78 v.
[59] LT 201.

turn for the worse. "The day before she could no longer stand on her feet," Marie of the Trinity later testified, "she still came to evening recreation. When Thérèse entered the common room, her breathing oppressed, burning with fever, she came and sat on her heels beside me. She whispered to me: *'I'm coming next to you so you can guard me. I feel that I no longer have the strength to carry on a conversation; you should look as if you are talking to me so that others won't start to speak to me. I confess to you that I do feel very sick, but I don't want to say so yet; Mother Agnes of Jesus would have such a hard time with it! ... Last night I needed more than half an hour to go back up to my cell: I had to sit down on almost every step of the stairs to recover my breath. When I arrived in my cell, I had to make what seemed enormous efforts to undress by myself; I thought for a moment I wouldn't be able to make it. If you only knew to what state of powerlessness illness reduces you.'"[60]* This episode probably took place at the end of May, the time when Thérèse had to abandon the community recreations.

The separation begins

Marie of the Trinity was pulled out of her employment as assistant infirmarian because Mother Marie de Gonzague held that she should no longer be in contact with the sick Thérèse, for fear of possible contagion. Thérèse sent several very short notes to her youngest novice in order to encourage her to accept the decision. On June 6, she wrote to her: *"I understand very well your sorrow at not being able to speak to me any more, but be assured that I am also suffering from my helplessness. Never have I felt so keenly that you hold an immense place in my heart."*[61]

As was often the case with Thérèse, profound reflections alternated with pleasant words in her notes. Thus in one note Thérèse first asked her friend to obtain for her the grace to die

---

[60] CRM 66-67.
[61] LT 242.

of love: "*I don't count on my illness, it's too slow a guide. I count only on love: ask the good Jesus that all the prayers being offered for me may serve to increase the Fire that must consume me.*" Then right afterward, Thérèse cheered up her companion by mimicking Fr. Baillon, one of the community's confessors, who had a very particular way of asking his penitents: "Do you regret your sins?" Thérèse ended her note: "*I believe you will not be able to read this; I do regret, but I have only a few minutes.*"

Brief encounters

They met less often now, but Thérèse showed her loving affection with even greater spontaneity. One day in June, Marie of the Trinity noticed the sick nun in her little wheelchair under the chestnut trees. Thérèse made a sign for her to come closer.

"Oh! no," the novice answered her. "We will be seen and I don't have permission." And she went to cry in the hermitage of the Holy Face. How surprised she was after just a few moments to see Thérèse sitting next to her on a tree stump.

"*I am not forbidden to see you,*" Thérèse said to her. "*Since I am dying, I want to console you!*" Then laying the novice's head upon her heart, Thérèse began to wipe away her tears. And as Marie of the Trinity begged the sick nun — who was trembling with fever — to get back into her wheelchair, Thérèse replied to her: "*Yes, I'll get in, but not before you make me smile!*"[62]

On July 8, Thérèse was moved permanently to the infirmary of the Holy Face. But it is said that the sick nun had an inscription placed on the door: "Forbidden for sad people to enter!" A note to Marie of the Trinity from this period began with these words: "*My dear little sister, I don't want you to be sad. You know what perfection I dream about for your soul.*"[63]

---

[62] CSM 55.
[63] LT 249.

On July 15, the evening before the feast of Our Lady of Mount Carmel, Marie of the Trinity said to the sick nun: "If you would die tomorrow after Communion, it would be such a beautiful death that I would be consoled in all my sorrow!"

Thérèse answered spiritedly: *"To die after Communion! On a great feastday! Oh! no, this isn't how I wish to die! This would be an extraordinary grace that would discourage all the little souls, because they couldn't imitate that. They must be able to imitate everything about me!"*[64]

A month later, at the end of August, when Thérèse was much sicker, Marie of the Trinity obtained permission to sit with her for half an hour. With her usual frankness, the young professed — she was only twenty-three years old, "with a child-like character" — confessed to the sick nun her need to play, to distract herself. *"Ah! how well I understand you,"* replied Thérèse, *"I would be exactly the same in your place! I give you the task of distracting yourself as much as possible. I even order you to go to the novitiate attic — in order that no one see or hear you — and to play there with the top that I gave you at Christmas. You need to do this!"*[65]

Thérèse had made an "illustrated book, full of entertaining stories," which the novice offered to her one day. *"How can you think this book could interest me?"* — the sick nun replied — *"I am too close to my eternity to want to distract myself."*[66]

Her remarks were often true sisterly corrections. Even on her sick bed, Thérèse did not lay down her weapons. *"A soldier has no fear of combat and I am a soldier,"* she remarked on July 8 to her godmother, concerning a novice who tired her a lot. After having scolded this novice, she added, *"Didn't I tell you that I would die, weapons in hand?"*[67] [from Thérèse's poem *Mes armes*].

Thérèse's firmness corresponded to the measure of her as-

---

[64] CSM 18.

[65] CSM 57.

[66] CRM 103.

[67] DE, pp. 693, 656.

pirations for her "doll." She wanted her to be "exactly the same" as herself and she wanted to be "proud" of her till the last day.[68]

On August 12, 1897, Thérèse wrote for her novice with a trembling hand, on the back of an image of the Holy Family, this final legacy, this final good-bye: *"To my dear little sister. Souvenir of her twenty-third birthday. May your life be all humility and love, that you may soon come to where I am going: into the arms of Jesus.... Your little sister, Thérèse of the Child Jesus of the Holy Face."*[69]

The death of a saint

During the last weeks, on the rare occasions when Marie of the Trinity had permission to enter the infirmary, she witnessed the martyrdom that Thérèse was undergoing.

One day — very probably at the end of August — she was present in the infirmary when Sr. Marie of the Sacred Heart [Marie] came to bring a cluster of grapes to Thérèse in the hope of relieving her thirst even a little bit. Thérèse then said to her "with kindness": *"To quench my thirst! Ah! it is over now! I will always, always be thirsty!"*

— "You should take some milk."

— *"The more I drink, the more I am thirsty; it is like pouring fire onto fire."*

Even in good health, the witness said, Thérèse could never digest milk and now she was reduced to being able to take nothing else.[70]

At the end of September on a laundry day, Marie of the Trinity went to see Thérèse, who said to her, smiling: *"I'm very glad to have been so sick today, to compensate for the fatigues that I can't share with you. Thus I have nothing to envy you about."*[71]

Three days before her death, again Marie of the Trinity

---

[68] CSM 56.
[69] LT 264.
[70] CRM 104.
[71] CRM 103-104. See CJ 7.27.4.

testifies, "I saw her in such agony that I was sorrowfully moved. She still made an effort to make me smile and, with a voice almost broken by suffocation, she told me: '*Ah! If I did not have faith, never could I bear so much suffering! I'm surprised that there aren't more atheists who take their own lives!*'

"Seeing her so calm and so strong in the midst of such a martyrdom, I couldn't hold back from telling her that she was an angel.

"'*Oh! no,*' she replied, '*I am not an angel. They're not as happy as I am.*'

"She wanted me to understand," remarked the witness, "that angels don't have the privilege of suffering to manifest their love."[72]

On September 29, Thérèse was at the very end of her suffering. Marie of the Trinity went to the infirmary but Thérèse was so exhausted that "after a few moments" she asked her "gently" to leave. As soon as she departed, Mother Agnes said to Thérèse: "Poor little one! she loves you so much!" Thérèse answered: "*Was I naughty to send her away?*" Her face then took on such an expression of sadness that Mother Agnes needed to reassure her.[73] This was the last encounter between Thérèse and her disciple.

Regarding Thérèse's last moments, here is the testimony that was given to us by Marie of the Trinity:

"The day of her death, after Vespers, I went to the infirmary where I found the Servant of God undergoing with invincible courage the throes of a most dreadful last agony. Her hands were totally purple; she held them together in anguish and cried out with a voice made loud and clear by the violence of pain: '*Oh! my God! ... have mercy on me! ... Oh! Mary! come to my help! ... My God... how I suffer! ... The chalice is full... full to the brim! ... Never will I know how to die!*'

---

[72] CRM 105.

[73] CJ 9.29.6.

"'Courage,' Mother Prioress said to her, 'you are reaching the end, just a little more and everything will be over.'

"'No, Mother, it is not over yet... I feel it clearly... I will suffer on like this, maybe for months!'

"'And if it were God's will to leave you so long on the cross,' our Mother continued, 'would you accept it?'

"With a tone of extraordinary heroism, she replied: 'I will it!' And her head fell back on the pillow with an expression so calm, so surrendered, that we could no longer keep back our tears....

"I left the infirmary, not having the courage to assist any longer at such a painful spectacle. I returned there only later with the community for the last moments and I witnessed her beautiful and long ecstatic look [regard] at the moment when she died, around 7 o'clock in the evening on Thursday, September 30, 1897."[74]

B) AFTER THE DEATH OF THÉRÈSE

Marie of the Trinity was only twenty-three years old when Thérèse died. In order to assimilate her teachings and carry out the fruits of them, a career of twenty-six years opened before her, years that she was going to pass in delightful memory of the one whom she more and more called "little Thérèse."

It seems opportune to distinguish two periods of her long lifetime:[75]

1897-1923: *In the radiance of Thérèse.*

In copying her written memories, in preparing her deposition for the beatification Process and in responding to the enormous amount of mail that came to Carmel, the former novice

---

[74] CRM 105-107.
[75] VT 87, p. 137.

was almost forced to go ever more deeply into Thérèse's doctrine and life.

1923-1944: *In resemblance to the Holy Face.*

One month before Thérèse's beatification, Marie of the Trinity fell gravely ill. Lupus slowly disfigured her face and gave her the appearance of a "leper," which is the name that she gave herself at the end of her life. She never stopped working in the radiance of Thérèse and found more and more in the contemplation of the Holy Face the strength to live her ordeal with true heroism.

1. In the radiance of Thérèse (1897-1923)

As she had done in 1893 for the Visitation in Mans,[76] Sr. Marie of the Angels sketched for the Carmel in Dijon, in August 1901, a portrait of each of the Carmelites of Lisieux. Here is the one about Marie our heroine:

> Sr. Marie of the Trinity (age 27). The rogue of Carmel! Never feels embarrassed by anything and knows perfectly how to pull herself out of any affair, feeling herself accompanied on her joyous path by her angel-guide, Sr. Thérèse of the Child Jesus, to whose special guidance she owes the good fortune of being a Carmelite. Still now, at any moment, she feels the assurance of Thérèse's sensitive and constant protection and remembers with joy that from heaven above Thérèse does not abandon her little game of ninepins. She claims to be so happy that she feels she will one day die of joy.

A marginal note indicates that she is the first employee in the baking of altar bread and that this "novice of our little saint"

---

[76] CG II, p. 1171 ff.

was "the little rabbit of whom Thérèse speaks in a letter to Céline."[77]

Already in this text of 1901, we find the two main traits which characterized the personality of Sr. Marie of the Trinity until her death: open joyfulness and a very vivid feeling of being accompanied on her earthly pilgrimage by her former novice mistress.

The memory of Thérèse in Carmel

We have already seen[78] the rapid development of the worldwide devotion to "Little Thérèse," to "the Little Flower," as Fr. Thomas Taylor said, this young Scottish priest who, passing by Lisieux in May 1903, there initiated the first idea of a canonization process. He hadn't expected the response of Thérèse's religious sisters: "But Father, how many Carmelites should we then canonize?"

In spite of the unexpected spread of the *Story of a Soul*, and the mail that brought every day an echo of Thérèse's increasing influence, the Carmelites kept a cool head. They so little imagined a possible canonization that they didn't even keep these letters, in order to avoid responding to them in a stereotyped way.

The Martin sisters couldn't imagine that their benjamin would one day be "raised to the altars." When in 1909, the prioress of the Visitation in Caen went into the monastery garden to inform Léonie [Sr. Françoise-Thérèse] that the canonization process was being seriously considered, Léonie continued to spread out the linen and exclaimed: "Thérèse! She was very kind! But a saint! Really!"[79]

Marie of the Trinity shared this point of view. She certainly

---

[77] LT 167 (trans.).

[78] *In the Footsteps of Thérèse*, O.E.I.L., 1983, pp. 17-68.

[79] St.-J. Piat, *Léonie*, Lisieux, 1966, p. 147.

had much veneration for Thérèse, she considered her like a saint and prayed to her as one. But she never thought of canonization. In those days people had a completely different idea about "canonizable" holiness. Sanctity was seen haloed with extraordinary charisms, accompanied by sensational mortifications. Little by little, however, the idea of canonization made headway, even in Carmel. On June 6, 1905, the same day that Pius X announced the beatification of the sixteen Carmelites of Compiègne, the mail brought a petition from a seminary in Tournai, pleading for the introduction of the Cause of Thérèse of the Child Jesus. This time the Carmelites could not help but see a sign in this coincidence. The martyrs of the Revolution seemed to be saying to them, "Now that our Cause is settled, take care of our little sister: it's her turn!"

What most surprised the Carmelites in this year 1905, was the great number of postulants who, captivated by the *Story of a Soul*, sought to enter the Carmel of Lisieux. Since Teresa of Avila had expressly wished for small numbers in her communities, they were obliged to send many of them to other Carmels.

The Carmelites of Lisieux were obviously very happy that they had known "little Thérèse," who was receiving more and more admiration from all over the world. The majority however, had not truly discovered her — and "valued" her! — until 1898. "Seven-eighths of the community who lived with our little queen did not really know her except through the *Story of a Soul*," wrote Marie of the Trinity on May 3, 1908.[80]

She herself did not wait such a long time to appreciate her; she had lived so close by her side for more than three years! But she had the impression of living with Thérèse once again, after her entrance into heaven: "I feel her even closer to me," she wrote the same day, "than when we were together. When she was on earth, I had to endure sharing her with many other people, but now she is with me entirely and I don't have to share

---

[80] Germaine, 5/3/08.

her anymore. I think this is the privilege of all those who are part of the legion of 'little souls,' of whom she is the queen."

Various works of the young nun

Above all, we are not going to imagine a Carmel that thought only about Thérèse. Marie of the Trinity herself, who — as we will see later on — had spent a lot of time copying out Thérèse's texts or those concerning testimony about her, also spent even more time copying entire pages of Holy Scripture or the great spiritual authors. From 1902 on, ignorant of the existence of the Gospel concordance, she put together one unified version of the four Gospels. It became a magnificent book in calligraphy, 293 pages long, which she offered on January 21, 1903, to Mother Agnes for her feast. It was entitled, *History of the Life of Our Lord Jesus Christ according to the four Gospels*, and contains in an appendix the list of all the Gospel parables, the miracles and the table of "Gospels which are read during the Year." From this she made several manuscript copies. She transcribed for herself in the same way, a notebook (140 pages, small format) of extracts from the Old Testament, according to a translation by M. Crampon.

Her well-formed letters were her preferred choice for the important copies and her agile pen delighted, at the first free moment, to revive the thoughts of the authors. In the archives of Carmel there are eleven of these notebooks, veritable anthologies of spiritual authors. John Chrysostom (442 pages) and Bernard of Clairvaux (190 pages) take up the greatest part of the set, but we also find there Teresa of Avila, John of the Cross, the Curé of Ars, Fr. Pichon, Francis de Sales, Bossuet, Tauler, Francis of Assisi, Dom Gueranger, Dom Chautard, Msgr. Gay, the Venerable Cottolengo, Sr. [later Bl.] Elizabeth of the Trinity, etc. We have seen above that she had likewise made notes of the retreat given by Fr. Boulanger, O.P., to the Carmel of *l'avenue de Messine* in 1892.

Her memory easily kept track of all this spiritual booty so that when someone was searching for any reference whatsoever, they had recourse to her. In order to conserve as faithfully as possible the sermons which she heard, she used shorthand, according to the Prévost-Delaunay method.

The mail

Marie of the Trinity had another occupation, as fascinating as it was passionate. Her facility at composition caused her to be counted among the "writers" — that is how the team of Carmelites were humorously called who took care of the mail coming to the monastery, which grew more abundant every day. The correspondents asked the Carmelites to pray to Thérèse for such intentions as: conversion, or the healing of a child or a husband or wife, reconciliation of a family, etc. There were requests for intercession, but also letters of thanksgiving. In 1909, the letters averaged twenty to thirty a day; by 1911, fifty. In the following years, the daily flow exceeded two hundred[81] and rose to four hundred in 1914. During the war, despite the postal difficulties, they still received five hundred letters a day.

One can imagine the work of the "secretaries"! It was sometimes wearisome, but Marie of the Trinity was given body and soul to the Cause of Thérèse. She sang this for Mother Agnes' feast on January 21, 1911:

> For our little Thérèse
> I devote myself with love.
> In working thus, without stopping,
> Ah! how time to me seems short![82]

Among the correspondents, many communities wanted to

---

[81] Germaine, 1/6/13.
[82] VT 85, p. 74.

be in touch regularly with the Carmel of Lisieux, and especially with the one who had been Thérèse's "little Mother." Real friendships thus developed between Mother Agnes and certain prioresses. This was particularly true with the prioress of Angers.

The other side of it was that Mother Agnes was often buried under the mail. Frequently she entrusted the work to other members of the "writing team." Marie of the Trinity was assigned to answering the letters from Angers. She thus became the regular correspondent with a young professed of this Carmel, Sr. Germaine Leconte, a younger cousin of Thérèse.[83]

This correspondence — which extended over more than six years — sheds a lot of light on the activities and personality of Marie of the Trinity who, in response to an enthusiastic disciple, willingly became the apostle and witness of the "Little Way." In this epistolary exchange, the former novice was sometimes led to give autobiographical details about Thérèse.[84]

At the service of pilgrims

It was also necessary to respond to the unceasing and increasing requests of pilgrims or the letter writers who asked for relics[85] and photographs of Thérèse. Again Marie of the Trinity

---

[83] Captain Martin, the paternal grandfather of Thérèse, and Germaine's maternal grandfather were first cousins. The Carmel of Angers has meticulously kept this mail coming from Lisieux. The first letter that was kept dates from 1908, the period when the "cult of Thérèse exploded into the universe" (August 12). The last one dates from 1917. The following year, Sr. Germaine had to leave her Carmel for a sanitarium located in Bégard (Côtes-du-Nord) which was run by the Sisters of the Good Savior of Caen. She died on April 17, 1943.

[84] Thus, in her letter of Nov. 26, 1916, she indicates that Thérèse didn't like the photograph in which she was shown performing her duties as sacristan (VTL 40), whereas she liked very much the "same subject which is cropped close to the veil" (VTL 39). "Little Thérèse said that this was the best of her photographs" (VT 88, p. 307).

[85] Sr. Marie of the Trinity made little packets containing some of Thérèse's hair. See the note to Mother Agnes, 1/21/06.

made a practical contribution: she contacted the publishers, handed on orders, confirmed packages upon their arrival and handled the bookkeeping. So in 1912, with the beginning of an administration center across from the monastery, her range of tasks was not at all diminished — much to the contrary! It brought additional charges to her work load, but the profits went to maintain the "till for beatification."[86]

In August of 1911, Marie of the Trinity saw her youngest sister, Marguerite-Marie, already twenty-eight, arrive as a postulant. But the attempt was short-lived: at the end of four months, the postulant had to rejoin her family. Several years later, on the recommendation of Mother Agnes, she made contact with the monastery of the Visitation in Caen, where the penances had a reputation of being less austere than those of Carmel. She successfully entered there and, on January 29, 1917, received the habit of a novice under the name Marguerite-Agnes. In choosing this name, she acknowledged her recognition of the one who had helped her to see clearly into her vocation.[87]

Yet another connection was established between the Carmel of Lisieux and the Visitation in Caen, since Thérèse's sister Léonie entered there definitively in 1899. Marie of the Trinity was happy to be even a little bit more similar to Thérèse now: she too had one of her sisters as a Visitation nun in Caen.

On October 1, 1913, Mme. Castel, now a widow, and Michaëlle, one of her sisters, installed themselves in *Les Buissonnets* and were charged by Carmel to receive the growing number of pilgrims who desired to visit this house where Thérèse had spent her youth. It is easy to perceive the joy of Marie of the Trinity when, in parlor visits with her family, she received an echo of what the pilgrims were saying at *Les Buissonnets*, notably their reliance on the intercession of little

---

[86] Germaine, 5/1/12.
[87] Obituary of Sr. Marguerite-Agnes (Archives of the Visitation in Caen).

Thérèse. And Thérèse certainly took on some of the intentions they had written there in the "golden book."

Mme. Castel died at *Les Buissonnets* on June 23, 1915. Michaëlle continued to assure the pilgrims of welcome for about ten years, until the day when she was replaced by her sister Violette.

The faithful were coming from all over the world. Among them were an increasing number of bishops from Africa or America who were profiting from their *ad limina* visit to the Holy See to make a detour via the Norman city;[88] they wanted to kneel at Thérèse's grave and asked to spend a few moments inside of "her" Carmel. During that period, Msgr. Lemmonier, the local ordinary, usually granted this authorization. Lucky bishop-pilgrims, first links in a long chain of prelates who asked for the favor to pray in their turn in the same places where Thérèse had wondrously discovered all the tenderness of God. It suffices to recall some names: Cardinal Pacelli (Pope Pius XII), Cardinal Roncalli (Pope John XXIII), Pope John Paul II.

But let us return to the whereabouts of the bishops within the enclosure of Carmel in 1913. "All this makes us happy," wrote Marie of the Trinity, "but it also takes a lot of time." And it is understandable that she added: "It is a marvel that we can do all this while maintaining our religious life."[89]

Daily life in the monastery

For daily life in the monastery did continue, peaceful, austere, devout, with its daily rhythm of choral chanting and household activities. Marie of the Trinity, who was very skillful with her hands, worked equally well in the bookbinding studio as in the making of altar bread. Her relaxation consisted in changing her activities.

---

[88] Germaine, 5/28/11.
[89] Germaine, 1/6/13.

Excellent organizer that she was, Mother Agnes endeavored to balance the atmosphere of her hard-working beehive by enhancing the community celebrations. She didn't stint on poems, composing new verses for each feast which Marie of the Trinity — again, her! — recopied into a notebook of 236 pages!

Marie of the Trinity delighted in acknowledging how precious to her were Mother Agnes' care and tenderness. "I find you so merciful," she wrote to her on June 18, 1905, "that it seems to me that God couldn't be more so." "Oh! how much I love you!" she wrote to her fifteen years later. "My love for you and my little Thérèse are equal: this is no small thing to say."

Is this flattery? We don't think so. Under a form a little bit exaggerated, Marie of the Trinity expressed quite simply her profound affection: after having been Thérèse's second mother, Mother Agnes had become her own mother by becoming her prioress. Besides, Marie of the Trinity liked to remind her that since she was the first one to enter Carmel during her term as prioress, she was in some manner her "first daughter."

Depositions for the Processes

We will see in the appendix how the former novices were requested to give their testimony about Thérèse (p. 139ff.). We can say at this point that the year 1910 became a particularly laborious one for Marie of the Trinity. She dedicated long hours to the deposition she had to make during the first canonical Process, which opened on August 3, 1910, and her testimony was heard in March 1911.

Thus she was led to rethink the "Little Way," of which she gave a magnificent shorter version to Sr. Germaine on May 25, 1910: "I really think that this is the first time since the creation of the world that someone is being canonized a saint who has done nothing extraordinary: no ecstasies, no revelations, no mortifications which frighten little souls like ours. Her whole life can be summed up in one word: she loved God in all the ordinary actions of common life, performing them with great faithfulness. She always had a great serenity of soul, whether in her suffering or in her joyfulness, because she took everything as coming from God."

Marie of the Trinity was also charged with the classification of everything that was being received about Thérèse, deserving to be called by Msgr. Teil, vice-postulator of the Cause, "the Mother-archivist."[90]

Some extraordinary events

Even though the Church was preparing to canonize "a saint who has done nothing extraordinary" and who knew "neither ecstasies nor revelations," the Carmelites were obliged to recognize that since the death of Thérèse, many baffling things had happened. The mail never stopped bringing its share of marvels: Marie of the Trinity gives an echo of them in some of her letters. For instance, a seminarian in Issy-les-Moulineaux told about an appearance of Thérèse to him on the night of December 11-12, 1911, without his knowing that the next day the beatification Process was closing in Bayeux. Why did Thérèse tell him: *"Today in Bayeux, there is a grand celebration in my honor... I will send down a shower of roses"*?[91]

From time to time it was even inside the monastery that some strange things were happening. In September 1910, a few days after the first exhumation of Thérèse's remains, a very strong aroma of roses penetrated the house. It turned out that it was emanating from some rotten boards which were in a cor-

---

[90] "I have much, much work, but I am always seconded by my little subprioress who is very intelligent and also by Sr. Marie of the Trinity whom Msgr. de Teil calls the Mother-archivist. This amuses us: she is a novice of Thérèse and he thinks that she is an old religious, seventy years of age" (Letter of Mother Agnes to Léonie, 3/30/10).

[91] Germaine, 12/27/11. The name of the seminarian was Louis Expert (d. 1956).

ner and which were none other than some of the debris from the exhumed coffin.

Without "seeing the devil everywhere," the Carmelites were nevertheless obliged to think that the devil was sometimes interfering. This is what Marie of the Trinity told Sr. Germaine on January 6, 1913: "Last December 12, the day before the newspapers published the Vatican approval of Thérèse's writings, we were finishing Lauds in choir when suddenly we heard a dreadful noise coming from Sr. Thérèse's choir stall. We asked ourselves anxiously what this could mean. The key to the mystery was given to us the next morning when we found out about the good news and, some days later, we learned about the evil plots of some influential enemies of our little saint who were trying to suppress or at least retard this first triumph. By his hubbub, the devil made us hear the roar of his defeat."

A fervent disciple

Marie of the Trinity thought about Thérèse so often that frequently she dreamed of her. And since Mother Agnes was very interested in this genre of "nocturnal consolations," Sr. Marie of the Trinity recopied in 1904 the eight most important dreams since her childhood, as a way to please her prioress. This added another notebook to the collection of the young professed.[92]

The last dream she related is dated September 1904. We are giving large extracts of it here because of the profound influence it exercised on her entire life. In 1942, two years before her death, she confided to Sr. Marie of the Redemption, the real archivist of the Lisieux Carmel, that the memory of this dream sustained her a lot in the great ordeal of her health:

---

[92] VT 78, pp. 141-145. See VT 85, pp. 72-73.

We started a novena to Sr. Thérèse to obtain the healing of her cousin, Sr. Marie of the Eucharist [Marie Guérin]. During the following night I dreamed that the cousin said in agony to Mother Agnes: "Don't be sad. If you hear Thérèse's voice after my death, this will be a sign that I went straight to heaven." In fact, immediately after her death I saw her quite nimbly and rapidly crossing the tree-lined path of a beautiful garden. Then I heard Thérèse's voice saying to us: "Rejoice, all of you; she is happy with me forever in heaven."
Marie of the Trinity asked Thérèse: "When will it be my turn? And I, will I go straight to heaven? Am I acceptable to God?" Thérèse said not a word, but from her countenance [regard] the former novice knew that she must banish all fear from her soul. Thérèse made her to understand that on earth, Sr. Marie of the Eucharist often feared that God rejected her; it seemed to her that she did nothing and that all her suffering was useless. But it was this very condition that gave her all her merit and that purified her. The imperfections for which she could be reproached had not prevented her from going straight to heaven. Unknown to her, her failings were made up for through the painful privation of spiritual consolations.
This dream, concluded Marie of the Trinity, became like a grace for my soul, because it made me appreciate more the merit that we gain when we have to love Jesus in the night of faith.

We will see further on that Marie of the Trinity was not content to just dream about Thérèse: she truly followed her "Little Way," without consolations.

A fresh fidelity

The disciple never felt obliged to copy her novice mistress in thinking or in canonizing all her formulas. A bit humorously, she sometimes liked to take a counterpoint to a certain phrase of Thérèse. Thérèse had said to her one day, in reference to the moral sufferings endured by her little Mother: *"The saints who suffer never make me feel pity"* (see p. 105). Marie of the Trinity remembered that in 1911, when the subprioress and mistress of novices, Sr. Isabelle of the Sacred Heart, had begun to vomit blood, she had mischievously added: "As for me, I believe that in heaven I will have pity on the saints who suffer; they could have recourse to me! In the meantime, if you know anybody who is suffering, would you please point her out to me so that she may have pity from us! We will pray a fervent novena for her."[93]

But this did not keep her from later writing these lines: "My memories of Thérèse are sufficient for my prayers and I know that God does not ask anything else from me but to follow the 'Little Way' upon which Thérèse guided my first steps. Oh! how I love this little way! Also, I do everything I can not to swerve from it; it is so easy to make a detour that you have to pay constant attention in order to stay with it. But when I manage to do so, what peace, what a foretaste of heaven!"

No, the desire to imitate her "beloved little Thérèse" and to follow her "Little Way" never deteriorated into a servile or scrupulous imitation. Thus, on her 32nd birthday, she had absolutely no idea that one day she would become ill for a long time, as Thérèse had been. Like Thérèse and Teresa of Avila, she wanted to die *"weapons in hand,"* but she did not see herself brutalized by several months of illness:

"Oh! how I would like to fall on the field of battle, weapons in hand! Such is the death that I long for. This frightens me the least, and truly I don't understand that it is so little desired by souls who are, like us, totally given to God.

"How is it that people are more attracted to die of illness? You are so damaged several months prior to death, without being able to pray or to breathe, surrounded by Sisters with

---

[93] Germaine, 6/28/11.

heartbroken expressions on their faces, chanting prayers with mournful voices to make you die of sadness and fear!...

"I'd rather find myself all of a sudden, without knowing how, in the arms of God, taken by him in the midst of whatever I am doing in my religious life. Don't I do everything for him? Every moment, I am working for the sole purpose of gaining his Love the more. Well! I am confident that he will have pity on my good will and take me away with him when he will find me at my best. He who loves me infinitely more than I love him, will never take me in a moment of imperfection, much less of sin. Oh! no! his merciful Love to which I have surrendered myself is not capable of doing such a thing! Besides, his little queen is there to be on the lookout, and in her maternal pride she will very quickly throw all her supply of roses upon her doll, which will forever cover all her faults and make her sublime.

"It sometimes occurs to me, after a good act of virtue, to say to Thérèse: 'What are you waiting for to take me away? You must not put it into your head that I will ever do better; you miss a wonderful opportunity!'

"I believe she hopes to be tugged even more by her doll, since she turns a deaf ear! While waiting, I will surrender myself to God, full of confidence, not caring about anything else than to please him in all things."[94]

Totally surrendered to the good will of God, Marie of the Trinity won't be "detoured" when Thérèse comes and takes her by the hand to invite her to follow an unexpected path — that of a long calvary!

The celebrations at Lisieux

It is easily imaginable with what joy the Carmelites gathered for the festivities that were organized in their chapel on the occasion of Thérèse's beatification and canonization. On

---

[94] Agnes, 8/12/06.

March 26, 1923, the day of the solemn transference of Thérèse's relics, Marie of the Trinity suddenly remembered a dream that Thérèse had confided to her about a year before her death:

"Last night during the great silence, I was thinking about my approaching death; then I fell asleep for a moment. In this half-sleep, I found myself in the middle of a field that resembled a cemetery. The hawthorns were blossoming, the birds were singing, I saw many people celebrating. It was like a day of triumph! And I said to myself: 'But what is this all about? For whom is this feast? Yet it is a burial.'... And in spite of everything, I suddenly sensed it was my own burial. This dream seems quite mysterious to me and I can't help thinking that sooner or later we will understand its meaning."

Marie of the Trinity couldn't help but see in the day's events the realization of the predictions in Thérèse's dream. Her mortal body was indeed transferred from the cemetery to Carmel in the midst of a festive crowd under a spring sun and along a road bordered by blooming hedges.[95]

2. In the resemblance of the Holy Face (1923-1944)

A long Way of the Cross

Thérèse had foretold her beloved disciple that there are no roses without thorns. In the month preceding the celebrations of the beatification, in February 1923, Marie of the Trinity contracted pneumonia. A little later, a spot of tubercular origin appeared on the back of her head. It was lupus. It slowly covered her whole face and made her look like a "leper" — as she described herself during the last eight years of her life.

---

[95] CSM 47.

A "little mama" and godmother for the Work of Fr. Brottier

We remember that Victor Castel, the father of Marie of the Trinity, had helped Fr. Roussel with the Work he had founded in the service of the poor children in Paris: "The Work for First Communion" soon became "The Work for Apprentices." One of his sons, Joachim-Léon, had remained in contact with the Work, in that he provided them regularly with coal.

Now, in November 1923, a new director was named to be in charge of this Work: Fr. Daniel Brottier, of the congregation of Holy Spirit Fathers, a former missionary to Senegal and a great devotee of Thérèse. The very day that he took charge of the Work, he wrote to Mother Agnes to ask the Carmelites of Lisieux to join in praying a novena that he was making for his orphans — a novena he addressed to the one whom the pope has just proclaimed Blessed.

He had begun a project to build a chapel in honor of Thérèse in the very midst of the buildings on *rue de la Fontaine*. He also asked Thérèse for a "sign" that his project truly corresponded to the will of God: "I have asked Msgr. Dubois for an appointment to talk about *our* future chapel," he told Thérèse. "If you agree with *our* project, send me a sign: that I receive 10,000 francs before this visit. If not, I will renounce the project!"

The end of the novena arrived and the hour of the meeting approached. Still nothing…. The priest paced back and forth in the courtyard. Suddenly a woman rushed up to him: "Father, thank you! I asked you to pray for my son. He is cured! Take this! Here is an envelope!"

Fr. Brottier opened the envelope: 10,000 francs!

Thérèse shall have her chapel! This will be her first sanctuary in Paris.

All beaming, the priest took a taxi to the archbishop. Msgr. Dubois, to whom he confided his project, was rather astonished: "For a work involving young people, shouldn't you choose for a patron saint a young man like Aloysius Gonzaga, or Stanislaus Kostka?"

"You are right, of course," answered Fr. Brottier, "but it seems to me that the children who don't have mothers are in even greater need of a little mama!"

Cardinal Dubois gave the much desired authorization and, the same evening, after having explained to the children the reason for the novena, Fr. Brottier launched a campaign for the future chapel.[96] On the list of the very first subscribers was the name of Joachim-Léon Castel. The priest asked M. David, administrative director of the Work, whether he knew this benefactor: "I know him well," he answered, "he's our coal merchant!"

Curious, Fr. Brottier wanted to meet him. The meeting took place a few days later, which is how he learned about the existence of Sr. Marie of the Trinity, the coal merchant's sister. With great astonishment he learned that this Carmelite of Lisieux had been the novice of Sr. Thérèse of the Child Jesus, and that she had introduced Thérèse to the Work of the Orphans, of which he had just accepted the burden of leadership![97]

Fr. Brottier's joy was overwhelming! He wrote immediately to Sr. Marie of the Trinity and asked her to become the spiritual godmother of his Work. After that he asked Auguste Maillard, the sculptor for his chapel, to represent the former novice of Thérèse in the "Monument of Adoption" which he proposed to erect there. This is the memorial sculpture known so well to all who go today to pray in the Thérèsian sanctuary in the 16th district in Paris. It stands in the left transept and shows Marie of the Trinity bringing two boys to Thérèse. The first wears the arm band of the First Communicants and recalls the initial Work founded by Fr. Roussel; the second, in working clothes, represents the apprentices.

After 1923, the warm fraternal bonds between the Work

---

[96] Yves Pichon, *Le Père Brottier*, J. de Gigord, 1938, pp. 129-130.

[97] Deposition by Daniel Brottier about Joachim-Léon Castel in the beatification Process, *Summarium*, pp. 2-3. The first witness in the trial! This indicates his importance.

of the Orphans-Apprentices of Auteuil and the Carmel of Lisieux became more and more interwoven. As for Marie of the Trinity, she silently supported the Work in her prayers. Together with Fr. Brottier, she asked Thérèse to shower down and to multiply upon the orphanages "not only roses but banknotes!" And the great celestial friend of Fr. Brottier heard their prayer!

Let us again admire here the beautiful friendship that was established during these years between Sr. Marie of the Trinity and Fr. Brottier, both of whom chose to be Thérèse's disciples. We are fortunate to be able to see that there are many mansions in the Father's house [cf. Jn 14:2] and there are many ways to faithfully follow the "Little Way" marked out by Thérèse. On one and the same day, November 25, 1984, Pope John Paul II beatified two of her disciples: Sr. Elizabeth of the Trinity, the missionary Carmelite, and Fr. Brottier, the contemplative missionary.

Joy during hard times

In spite of the insidious development of her disease, Marie of the Trinity always lived the spirituality of the smile that Thérèse had bequeathed her. She continued her activities gracefully. Each year she prepared the calendar that suggested a thought of Thérèse for each day.[98] She continued to dedicate long hours to writing out quotations from spiritual authors, which Mother Agnes sometimes used for the exhortations she addressed to the community in the chapter room. Thoughts about the importance of joy and the prize of suffering obviously took pride of place:

> To sing one psalm with joy is worth more than reciting the whole psalter with sadness (St. Jerome).

---

[98] In March 1932, she was editing the calendar for 1933 (Agnes, 3/6/32).

No sadness! ... Perfection is to make each suffering die
under a smile (Msgr. Pagès).

Joy is in some ways a virtue: it indicates innocence and
bears witness to confidence in God. The face of this child
had that joyous look which would remain with the man
in a state of primal innocence (Life of St. Stanislaus
Kostka).

There is no wood more appropriate to nourish the fire of
love than the wood of the cross! (St. Ignatius).

God polishes a diamond with another diamond. This is a
great grace from God to suffer in little things all the time
(Fénelon).

Happy is the soul that God crushes, that God casts down,
from whom God pulls away all her strength, who feels
her weakness and who sees all her crosses increase still
from the interior cross of discouragement, without
which all the others weigh nothing (Bossuet).[99]

These thoughts are remarkably on line with Thérèse's
teachings: in order to suffer in the right way, it isn't at all necessary to suffer grandly! It's enough to suffer "in little things
all the time."

Marie of the Trinity needed very much to remind herself
of this. Her body became more and more curved so that soon
she couldn't do without her cane! The premature signs of age
contrasted very strangely with the playful turn of her comments.

The affection of Mother Agnes

The affectionate presence of her prioress was more than
ever a precious comfort to the sick nun. Marie of the Trinity
would knock at her door several minutes before the 5 p.m.
prayer and tell her: "Here is your little leper, dear Mother." This

---

[99] Notebook, 17 x 10 cm., pp. 356-357.

was not at all to complain about her condition but to delicately remind her prioress that she wanted to continue living her trial with her eyes fixed on the One whose Face had become an object of contempt during his Passion.

Then Mother Agnes would offer a spiritual bouquet to her beloved child. For example, during the last years it would be a thought from Sr. Marie of the Sacred Heart [Marie] who died on January 19, 1940. The sick nun would leave comforted, smiling with only half of her face, because the other half, all bandaged, was nothing more than a wound.

From time to time Mother Agnes took an image or cut out a design from an illustrated journal, added an inscription to it and sent it to her dear little "T" (the familiar abbreviation of Marie of the Trinity), to encourage her to live her trial in Thérèse's spirit:

> Next to an image of a black child guided by a protective hand it says: "I am going to heaven: Thérèse pulls me. I am black but I am beautiful [cf. Song 1:5] through suffering. It is Jesus who says this."
> Below a photo showing Thérèse sitting with her hands folded together, it says: "She keeps the wolf under observation and protects the lamb."

On another occasion Mother Agnes sent a note to the sick nun. Almost all of them have been destroyed. Sixty-six notes from Marie of the Trinity, on the contrary, have been found in Mother Agnes' papers, sent to her between 1905 and 1943. Most of them had been composed while Mother Agnes was making her annual retreat: it was then the custom that during the eleven days of strict silence, the prioress would keep in touch with her spiritual daughters by an exchange of letters.

To publish this correspondence, as intimate as it was, was no indiscretion. "The perfume emitted from the writings of the very first disciples is henceforth inseparable from the Rose who impregnated their hearts forever. It is the treasure of the Thérèsian family."[100] As Fr. Brottier noted with good reason: "These documents are of such straight realism, without excess and amazingly healthy. One can see in them how two of those who were closest to Thérèse live their religious life, helped by their memory of her, and spanning the most varied circumstances (the Process, beatification, canonization, other trials), in a manner that sheds light on what are called the real fruits of the teaching of Thérèse of Lisieux."[101]

These notes to Mother Agnes are the essential source to use when one wants to penetrate into the secrets of the joy that Marie of the Trinity maintained "until the end." We will use them largely in the third part of this work. They especially allow us to appreciate the foremost place of the Holy Face in her spiritual life. To please the Father in resembling the suffering Face of his beloved Son was unquestionably one of the great sources of her strength and her peace. That is where the cry of the heart comes from that she let burst forth in her note of June 6, 1939: "My God, if I would be a little less pleasing to you without my lupus, I much prefer to keep it in order to be completely pleasing to you."

The friendship of a Trappist

Another very deep friendship brought precious comfort to the former novice of Thérèse, that of Fr. Marie-Bernard, monk of the Trappist order of Soligny in the Orne valley. Very strong bonds were established between the Carmel of Lisieux and the Grand Trappist monastery ever since the day when Fr. Marie-Bernard had put all his talents as a sculptor into making several models of the statue of St. Thérèse. Responsible for purchasing one for Carmel, Marie of the Trinity began a frequent cor-

---

[100] VT 85, p. 63.
[101] *Glory and the Beggar*, Cerf, 1974, p. 231.

respondence with the monk, who also made several visits to the Carmel. These epistolary exchanges and meetings were the beginning of a real friendship. Fr. Marie-Bernard was an enthusiastic disciple of Thérèse; he endeavored to coin the "Little Way" into all sorts of parables, which he recounted marvelously. For example, Marie of the Trinity listened with much joy and carefully wrote down the parable of "the Poor Girl." This is the story of a young prince who employed all his charms to make the poorest girl in his kingdom love him. The girl actually refused his love. The prince forgave her and succeeded finally in winning the young girl's heart. Marie exulted: she was the poor girl whom the Lord loves to love in spite of her misery!

In 1940, the exchanges between the Carmelite and the Trappist became more and more profound. "Your words from our last parlor visit," she wrote to him on October 28, "have remained like a seed of consolation in the depth of my heart. God uses you as an instrument to do me much good; you will see that in heaven. Also for me it is a sweet task to pray for you; we both have something to give to each other and our union in heaven will be even more ravishing."

The end of Calvary

As much as she could, the sick nun still participated in all the common activities. She made sure she still had her turn as refectory reader and took part in the choir singing, holding her breviary in one hand and her inseparable cane in the other. When she had to renounce going to the Office of Matins [9 p.m.], she compensated by being the first one to arrive for morning prayer [5 a.m.].[102]

In 1941, her illness grew painfully worse. On July 21, she wrote to Fr. Marie-Bernard: "I am now disfigured on the left

---

[102] Obituary, p. 19.

side; the jawbone has a hard time to stay together and I have difficulty speaking." On April 24 of the following year, she excused herself to him for shortening her letter "because of her eye that made her suffer." And on August 2, she confided to him: "My lupus devours my head day and night. What continual acts of love and abandonment this causes me to make!" The continuing deterioration did not even give her time to rest!

The dressings of the wounds took longer and longer and became more painful. Sr. Germaine of the Sacred Heart took over from Sr. Madeleine who died in 1940. It required two hours every morning to redo them.

On December 8, 1943, the illness made a sudden leap that caused her vivid and piercing pain in the heel. "What do you expect?" Mother Agnes said to her. "It isn't astonishing that in helping the Holy Virgin as you do, to crush the head of the serpent, it tries to kill *you* by the heel also."[103] A sense of humor that Marie of the Trinity continued to appreciate.

Now she could be seen declining more and more. During the last weeks of her life, she needed thirty minutes to drink half of a little cup of liquid with the help of a straw.

At the beginning of January 1944, an epidemic of flu spread in the community. The sick nun was fatally hit. On January 6, she wrote to Fr. Marie-Bernard: "We are all sick with the flu more or less: as always, I got the big share of it: a 102° F. fever!"

On January 12, Sr. Marie of the Angels asked her: "What does Thérèse tell you in the midst of all of this?" "Ah! When you tell me, I'll repeat it for you. She has put me into the night of faith and has left me there. And I have no ambition to leave it!"[104]

On Saturday, January 15, she received the last sacraments. That afternoon Mother Agnes suggested some reassuring

---

[103] Obituary, p. 22. A reference to Genesis 3:15, used in the liturgy of the Immaculate Conception of the Blessed Virgin Mary, celebrated on December 8 (trans.).

[104] Autograph of Sr. Marie of the Angels: Visit to Sr. Marie of the Trinity, Jan. 12, 1944 (ACL).

thoughts to her, but she was content to say, "Sweet and humble Jesus!" The night that followed was calm. She was still conscious when she said to her nurse: "In heaven I will follow little Thérèse everywhere!" Those became her last words. On Sunday morning, after a short agony, she breathed her last breath at 11 o'clock.

Thus she was spared from participating in the painful exodus that took place in June 1944, as the bombardment began that accompanied the debarkation of the allied troops on the soil of Normandy. It is known in fact that the Carmelites of Lisieux lived for six weeks in the crypt of the basilica where they had taken refuge.

On January 19, several seminarians of the Mission of France came to take the coffin of the deceased to the door of the monastery in order to bring her into the chapel of Carmel where the funeral Masses were celebrated. The first prayer of absolution was given by a priest of the Work of the Orphans-Apprentices in Auteuil, the second by Msgr. Germain, pilgrimage director, and the third by Msgr. Fallaize, the famous Oblate of Mary who, after an apostolic life of service to the Eskimos, consecrated the last years of his priesthood to welcoming the pilgrims of Lisieux in the confessional.

The mortal remains of Sr. Marie of the Trinity were afterwards brought to the town cemetery, the same place where, between 1897 and 1923, thousands of Christians had come to pray at Thérèse's grave.

CHAPTER TWO

The Testimony of Marie of the Trinity[1]

A PROFOUND FAITH IN THE LOVE OF GOD

A great sun illuminated the whole life of Thérèse, the Lord's love for mankind:

> She spoke to me with such sweet unction about God's love for us, that often she was shedding tears.[2]
> She did everything with such perfection and with such a look of calm recollection that one could see she never lost the presence of God.[3]
> If Thérèse speaks little about her prayer, it is because she didn't have much more to say than: prayer of faith, very simple.[4]

HOLY SCRIPTURE

Thérèse drew from Scripture her acquaintance with the God who is "full of tenderness," chanted in psalm 102 [103], a psalm

---

[1] The French text employs three different typefaces to distinguish the speakers: (1) the author (regular roman), (2) St. Thérèse of the Child Jesus (regular italic), (3) Sr. Marie of the Trinity and all others (smaller roman). The same convention is used in presenting this English translation (trans.).

[2] CRM 24.

[3] CRM 2.

[4] Germaine, 7/17/09.

she often quoted.[5] She had bound for herself the four Gospels from her *Handbook for Christians*, in order to carry them always on her person to be able to frequently read a passage. She invited her novices to do likewise.[6] To support the advice she gave them, she often quoted a word from the Gospel.[7] One book of the Old Testament fascinated her in particular: the Song of Songs. Whenever she had the opportunity, she commented on one of its verses. One day she confided to Marie of the Trinity:

> *"If I had time, I would comment on the Song of Songs; I discovered in this book such profound things about the union of the soul with her Beloved."*[8]

THE HOLY FACE

God's love for mankind is expressed in a privileged way in the Passion of Christ, from whence comes Thérèse's very special devotion to the Holy Face:

> She was proud to bear his name. Very happy to see her two novices, Sr. Geneviève and me, share this devotion, she composed for the three of us a "Consecration to the Holy Face."[9]

She carried in her book of the four Gospels a photograph of Sr. Marie of St. Peter, the Carmelite of Tours who had contributed so much to spreading devotion to the Holy Face in the middle of the 19th century. From it she drew her ideas to write her very first poem.[10]

---

[5] BT, p. 84.
[6] Germaine, 9/27/08.
[7] CRM 9-10.
[8] CRM 10.
[9] CRM 12 - Pr 12, 8/6/96.
[10] *The divine rose*, 1/2/93 - CSM 35.

Nevertheless, since the Carmelite of Tours insisted on the task of making reparation for the abuses that had been committed against the Holy Face, Thérèse felt herself brought further, to *imitate* the model of humility that she contemplated there. A contemplation wholly nourished by chapter 53 of Isaiah: "His face was like one hidden from us; he seemed to us an object of contempt, the vilest of men." She often quoted this passage, adding:

"Oh! how I wish that my face was hidden like his, so that here on earth nobody could recognize me."

Asked point blank about the subject of her thoughts, she would often answer:

"Ah! how I would like to be unknown and counted for nothing!"

"It is a very just thing that someone despises us," she said another time, *"that someone shows us a lack of respect. It is to treat us as we deserve."*[11]

Let us not forget that in contemplating the Holy Face, Thérèse also loved to think of the gaze, full of tenderness, that Jesus unceasingly directed toward her. She alluded to this from the time of the first poem she composed for her companion, on the occasion of her taking the habit:

Your Son's indescribable gaze
has deigned to lower itself and descend on my poor soul:
I have been searching for his adorable Face
For it is in It that I want to hide myself.[12]

---

[11] CRM 80-82. The yearning to be "unknown and despised" dates from the beginning of Thérèse's religious life (See LT 95; A 71 r), under the influence of John of the Cross ("to suffer and to be despised"), the *Imitation of Christ* and above all Isaiah 53, which she discovered in 1899 (BT, pp. 130-132). It seems, meanwhile, that this desire was intensified in 1895-1896 (see PN 20, str. 2; PN 31, ref. 3 and str. 4). It is thus probable that this reflection of Thérèse's dates from 1896.

[12] PN 12, *It is close to you, Virgin Mary*, str. 3.

THE EUCHARISTIC MYSTERY

Thérèse's faith in this mystery was expressed by the joy and respect with which she prepared the sacred vessels for the next morning's Mass:

> One day I met her under the cloister; her contemplative mood astonished me. She seemed to be carrying something very precious that she sheltered carefully with her scapular. At the moment I went by her, she said to me in a low voice:
>
> *"Follow me, I am carrying Jesus!"*
>
> She was coming from taking away the little gilded plate from the communion table upon which she had discovered a fairly large particle of the Sacred Host. I followed her to the sacristy where, after she had put down her treasure, she made me kneel next to her to pray until she could give it back to the priest, to whom she had sent notice.[13]

But Thérèse never forgot the ultimate purpose of the Eucharistic presence: it is to give himself as nourishment that Jesus becomes present under the appearance of bread. That is why she suffered so much not to be able to receive Communion every day. Mother Marie de Gonzague didn't have the daring to follow the directives of Leo XIII, who encouraged religious superiors to allow daily Communion in their community. Also, Thérèse didn't want to deprive herself of receiving Communion on days when the Carmelites did have authorization:

> One such Communion day, as Thérèse was very tired, Mother Marie de Gonzague wanted to make her take some medicine before Mass. In her sorrow at missing

---

[13] CRM 7-8.

Holy Communion,[14] she implored her prioress in tears not to take it until after Mass. She explained her reasons so well that she obtained permission, and since this day, receiving Holy Communion was made a priority over everything else.[15]

Thérèse urged that Jesus was in her heart not only when he came in Holy Communion, but that he dwelt constantly within her as he had promised: "The one who eats my flesh and drinks my blood abides in me and I in him" (Jn 6:56). Since she couldn't receive Communion as often as she desired, she asked the Lord to remain in her heart from one Communion to the next. She expressed this prayer in her Act of Offering:

"I know it is true, O my God, that the more you desire to give yourself, the more you make me desire you. I feel infinite desires in my heart and it is with confidence that I ask you to come take possession of my soul. Ah! I cannot receive Holy Communion as often as I desire, but, my Lord, are you not all-powerful? Remain in me as in a tabernacle; don't ever withdraw yourself from your little host."[16]

She told me that nothing was impossible to the omnipotence of God and that he would not have inspired this request if he had not wanted it to be realized.

Marie of the Trinity was much more attentive to Thérèse's desire, since she herself had received the grace to feel the presence of Jesus in her heart during the entire day after her Offering to Merciful Love on December 1, 1895:

I was so flooded with graces on that beautiful day, the most beautiful day of my life, that all day long I experi-

---

[14] Taking medicine before Mass would have broken the law then in effect regarding the amount of time to fast before receiving Communion: nothing could be taken by mouth after midnight (trans.).

[15] CRM 9.

[16] CRM 30-31.

enced in a very tangible way the presence of the Eucharistic Jesus in my heart. I confided this to Sr. Thérèse of the Child Jesus, who was not at all surprised and answered me simply:

"Is God not omnipotent? If we so desire, it would not be difficult for him to make his sacramental presence in our souls remain from one Communion to the next. Through this extraordinary feeling that you experienced today, he wishes to give you the pledge that all the requests you have made of him in the Act of Oblation will be lavishly granted. You will not always enjoy these feelings, but their effects will be no less real. One receives from God as much as one hopes for."[17]

It is in this sense of the habitual presence of Jesus in the soul of the communicant that Thérèse interpreted two lines of a poem that she composed several months later, on May 31, 1896, feast of the Holy Trinity, for the feast of her novice:

You, the great God, whom all the heavens adore,
You live in me, a prisoner night and day.[18]

Sr. Thérèse of St. Augustine tried to tell Thérèse that she should have said, "You live *for* me," but Thérèse replied, while giving a knowing wink to Marie of the Trinity:

"No, no, I have said it well."[19]

During the apostolic Process for Thérèse's canonization Marie of the Trinity added:

---

[17] CSM 39.

[18] PN 31, 5.

[19] PO, p. 458. In her *Red Notebook*, in an undated note (written without doubt in 1935), Sr. Marie of the Trinity brought together two verses of May 31, 1896, with the reflection that Thérèse made to her on December 1, 1895, a reflection which she gives us here in another version: *"This extraordinary feeling that you experience is proof that God lavishly grants all that you ask of him. Yes, for his little 'victims of love,' he likes to make wondrous gifts which infinitely surpass their immense desires, but usually they labor in faith; otherwise they could not live. The Real Presence will not make itself felt, but it is no less existential. Nothing is impossible to the omnipotence of God and I am sure that he would not have inspired this request if he would not have wanted to realize it."*

She has never explained to me the manner of this presence and I don't think that she herself ever made an effort to find out what kind of presence this was.[20]

Let us point out that Thérèse's audacious insight anticipated in a marvelous way what contemporary theological thinking has rediscovered about the subject of the intimate presence of the risen Lord in the heart of the world. Since his resurrection from the dead, the humanity of Christ escapes all limitations of space and time. Christ had said explicitly to his disciples before completing the time of his post-resurrection appearances: "I will be with you until the end of time" (Mt 28:20). It is through his glorified body that the Word pours into our hearts his Holy Spirit, with whom this body has been completely imbued. When Paul wrote to the Galatians (2:20) that Christ lives in him, Paul was not coming from Holy Communion. But it is certainly true that the whole glorified Christ, true God and true man, lived in him.

This presence of Christ in the heart of the Christian is not a static presence. Christ exercises a greater and greater influence upon the soul that opens itself to him. Better yet, he changes it into himself. Thérèse often sang in her Eucharistic poems about this effect of Communion:

"Oh! what fortunate moment when, in your tenderness,
You come, my Beloved, to transform me into you."[21]

"We also are the hosts
That Jesus wants to change into himself."[22]

JOY ON ONE'S FACE

Since the Lord is so close, we don't have the right to be sad. Thérèse often came back to the task of being "always happy."

---

[20] PA, pp. 469-470.
[21] PN 32, 3.
[22] PN 40, 6.

One day when I was crying, she told me to try to get accustomed to not showing my little sufferings, adding that *"nothing made community life more depressing than emotional ups and downs."* I responded to her:
"You're right. From now on I won't cry anymore except with God; to him alone shall I confide my pains. He will always understand and console me."

"To cry in front of God!" answered Thérèse. *"Keep yourself absolutely from doing such a thing. You should appear even less sad in front of him than in front of creatures. Indeed! This good master has only us monastics to delight his heart. He comes to us to rest and to forget about the continual laments of his friends on earth, because most of the time on earth people are crying and groaning instead of recognizing the prize of the cross. And you want to do as common mortals do? [...] Frankly, this is not about disinterested love. It is for us to console Jesus, it is not up to him to console us. I know very well that he has such a good heart that when he sees you cry, he will wipe away your tears; but afterwards he will be very sad that he could not rest his divine head upon you. Jesus loves happy hearts. He loves a soul that is always smiling. When, then, will you know how to hide your pain from him, or to tell him singing that you are happy to suffer for him?"*[23]

This is why we are obliged to always keep a smile on our face:

• When we are alone.

She reproved me each time she saw me frowning or tensing my face:

"The face is the reflection of the soul: it should always be calm and serene like that of a little child who is always content, even when

---

you are alone, because you are constantly visible to God and the an-gels."[24]

• When we suffer.

> One day we were speaking about the good fortune of the martyrs and of our hope to become one because of the religious persecutions:

> *"As for me,"* she said, *"I already practice suffering joyously. For example, when I give myself the discipline [self-flagellation], I imagine myself to be under the blows of the executioners in order to confess my faith. The more I hurt myself, the more I wear a joyous expression. I do the same with all other bodily suffering: instead of letting my face tense with pain, I make a smile."*[25]

• Even and above all when we are humiliated.

> An old religious — we know that it was Sr. St. John the Baptist — could not understand why Sr. Thérèse of the Child Jesus was in charge of the novices, and made her feel it. One day, in the midst of recreation she said some bitter words to her, among others, that she had more need to conduct herself properly than to guide others. From afar, I witnessed the scene: the tenderness of the servant of God contrasted so starkly with her accuser's expression of rage, and I heard her reply:

> *"Ah! Sister, you are right, I am even more imperfect than you can imagine!"*[26]

Some days before she died, Thérèse came back again to the task of being serene. She asked her novice to again take up the

---

[24] CRM 14.

[25] CRM 61.

[26] CRM 81.

humble strategy that she had recommended to her before, to dry up her source of tears.

> Eight days before her death, I had wept one whole evening thinking of her approaching departure. She perceived this and said to me:

> *"You have been crying. Did you put the tears in the shell?"*

> I could not lie and my confession saddened her. She replied:

> *"I will be dying and I will not be tranquil about you if you do not promise me to follow my recommendation faithfully. This is of the greatest importance for your soul."*

> I gave my word, asking nevertheless for permission to cry about her death:

> *"Why do you want to cry about my death! Here are really useless tears. You should cry about my good fortune. But, after all, I have pity on your weakness and I permit you to cry for the first few days. But after that, you need to take the shell again."*[27]

MERCIFUL LOVE

Thérèse was inexhaustible about this subject. One day when Marie of the Trinity confided to her the fear she had that God would be angry with her because of her repeated imperfections, Thérèse said to her:

> *"Set your mind at rest. The one whom you have taken as your Spouse has certainly all the desirable perfections; but if I dare say, he has a great weakness at the same time: that is, to be blind! And there*

---

[27] CSM 55.

is a science that he doesn't know: arithmetic! These two great faults, which would be really regrettable deficiencies in a mortal spouse, make our Spouse infinitely lovable. If it were necessary that he see clearly, or he know how to calculate, do you think that in the presence of all our sins he wouldn't make us go back into nothing? But no, his love for us makes him perfectly blind! See for yourself! When the greatest sinner on earth repents of his offenses at the moment of death, and dies in an act of love, forthwith, without counting up the numerous graces that the unhappy person has abused, nor all his other crimes, God counts only his last prayer and receives him without any delay into his merciful arms."[28]

This is why the memory of our past faults must not overwhelm us. The embarrassment over the fact that we have sinned must give way to the bewilderment that we are so much loved:

"The rest of us," she would tell me, *"don't belong among those saints who cry over our sins: we take delight in them because they serve to glorify the mercy of God."*[29]

Thérèse was conscious of being unique in the manner of crying for joy in remembrance of her past faults. This audacity constituted an integral part of the very new "Little Way" that she felt was her mission to show to souls. Moreover, the joy we experience when we forgive in this way gives us a slight idea of the joy that dwells in the heart of God when we accept his forgiveness. One day, Marie of the Trinity couldn't accept an observation that Thérèse made to her. Shortly thereafter, when she acknowledged her faults, she saw how her companion's eyes brimmed with tears:

"If you only knew what is going on within me!" Thérèse said to her. *"No, I have never experienced so vividly with what love Jesus receives us when we ask him to forgive us after we have offended him.*

---

[28] CRM 17-18.

[29] CSM 50. Thérèse was conscious of being audacious in the manner of surrendering herself to the infinite mercy of the Lord (see LT 247).

Hardly had you begun to express your repentance to me that I felt for you more love than before. If such is the case with me, poor little creature that I am, what must God experience when the sinner returns to him? Faster than I could do it — because HE doesn't wait until the words come out of our lips — with the first movement of the repentant heart, not only does he pardon, forget and return his love to the sinner, but he loves him even more than before his failure. Ah! if I were alone, I would be sobbing. This is too much love!"[30]

Thérèse did not discover in books this "Little Way" of confidence and love:

"Where did this teaching of yours come from?" her novice asked her one day.

"It is God alone who has instructed me. No book, no theologian has taught me and nevertheless I feel at the bottom of my heart that I am in the truth. I have not received encouragement from anybody, and when the occasion did come to open my soul, I received so little understanding that I said to God, like St. John of the Cross: 'From now on, don't send me any messengers anymore, who don't know how to tell me what I desire.'"

— "If you had heard the sermons of Fr. Boulanger, provincial of the Dominicans in Paris, you would have been very much consoled!"

And Marie of the Trinity cited some of the preacher's phrases that exactly matched the teaching of the "Little Way." Thérèse then exclaimed:

"What consolation you give me! To know myself supported by an expert, a renowned theologian, gives me an incomparable joy!"[31]

---

[30] CRM 24-26.
[31] CSM 46.

In fact, it is in the Gospel that Thérèse discovered her "Little Way." Also it is a sure way:

"If I am leading you in error with my little way of love, don't be afraid that I would let you follow it for very long. I would appear to you soon in order to tell you to take another route. But if I don't return, believe in the truth of my words: one can never have too much confidence in God, who is so powerful and so merciful! One receives from him quite as much as one hopes for!"[32]

Thérèse expressed herself in the following testimony as if her death were already near. The reflection must therefore date from 1897. The *Red Notebook* even clarifies the circumstances. Thérèse asked Marie of the Trinity one day if, after her death, she would abandon the "Little Way."

"Surely not," she replied. "I believe in it so firmly that it seems to me that even if the pope would tell me that you have been deceived, I couldn't believe it."

"Oh!" responded Thérèse, *"One must believe the pope before all else. But don't be afraid that he will tell you to change the way; I won't give him time for that. Because if when I arrive in heaven I learn that I have led you into error, I will get permission from God to return immediately and inform you. Until then, believe that my way is certain and follow it faithfully."*[33]

Thérèse's desire was to reveal to everybody this infinite mercifulness of God. Had she not been accepted in Carmel, she would have entered a congregation specializing in the reception of "unfortunate girls," as they said in those days. Thérèse

---

[32] CSM 17.

[33] CRM 19-20. Let us pay attention to this last expression: "My way is certain" appears only in the testimony of Marie of the Trinity in the bishop's Process, in her deposition of March 1911. It is quite probable that she made her testimony coincide with the phrase that Thérèse had said to the prioress of the Carmel at Gallipolis when she appeared to her in the night of January 16, 1910: "My way is certain and I have not been mistaken in following it!"

knew their establishment in Lisieux, because she had more than once accompanied M. Martin, who used to bring to them the fish he had caught. To help Marie of the Trinity accept a humiliation, Thérèse confided to her one day:

"If I had not been accepted in Carmel, I would have entered a shelter in order to live there unknown and despised in the midst of the poor unfortunates. My happiness would have been to pass for one of them. I would have made myself the apostle of my companions, telling them what I think about the merciful love of God."

"But how would you have managed to hide your innocence from your confessor?"

"I would have told him that I had made a general confession before entering and that this protected me from mentioning it again."[34]

A PROFOUND HUMILITY

Humility before God, the spirit of a child: these are some of the attitudes that spring from this discovery of merciful Love.

When Jesus presented the child to us as a model, it is not by virtue of the child's innocence — the Christian does not live in nostalgic feelings about his lost innocence — but because of his fundamental powerlessness. A beloved powerlessness, because it is the ostensible reason for letting himself be carried on the shoulders of the Lord. The child does not do "evil": he knows his radical incapacity to escape from it all by himself.

"The privileges of Jesus are for the little ones," Thérèse said again and again.

She was inexhaustible when it came to talking about the

---

[34] CRM 80-82. A confidence that already supposed a great intimacy between them and which therefore must be dated between 1896-1897.

confidence, the abandonment, simplicity, honesty and humility of little children:

> "I would like to have more strength and energy to practice virtue," Marie of the Trinity said to her one day.
>
> *"And if God wants you to be weak and powerless like a little child, do you think you will be less worthy?... Consent, then, to stumble at every step, even to fall, to carry your cross feebly. Love your powerlessness; your soul will draw more profit than if, supported by grace, you achieve with a certain flair heroic acts which fill your soul with personal satisfaction and selfish pride."*[35]

Another time, when the novice was saddened by her short-comings, Thérèse answered her:

> *"There again, you are deserting the Little Way! The pain that knocks down and discourages comes from self-love; the supernatural pain restores courage, gives a new energy for doing good. One can be happy to feel weak and miserable because the more one recognizes this condition humbly, while waiting altogether gratuitously for God without any merit on our part, the more God lowers himself to us in order to give us abundantly of his gifts with magnificence."*[36]

The child of God knows herself incapable of climbing all by herself the rough steps of perfection. She must let herself be carried in the arms of her God. But this does not eliminate the need for human effort. That is where the famous parable comes from that Thérèse invented from her own childhood memories in Alençon:

> *"You make me think of the very little child who starts to hold herself up but does not yet know how to walk. Wanting absolutely to climb to the top of the stairs to find her mother again, she lifts her little foot to finally climb the first step. Useless labor! She always falls with-*

---

[35] CRM 83-84.
[36] CRM 84-86.

out making any advance. Okay! Consent to be this little child. Through practicing all the virtues, keep lifting up your little foot in order to clamber up the stairs of holiness. You will not even get to the first rung, but God asks nothing of you except your good will. From the top of the stairs he looks down at you with love. Soon, won over by your ineffective efforts, he will come down himself and, taking you in his arms, he will take you away into his kingdom forever, where you will never have to depart from him. But if you give up lifting your little foot, he will leave you on earth for a very long time."[37]

"The happy day when Jesus will himself come down to carry you away in his arms," Thérèse said another time, *"will you be more advanced by having clambered up five or six steps by your own strength? Is it more difficult for Jesus to take you from the bottom rather than from the middle of the stairs? There is yet another advantage for you not being able to mount up: that is, to remain your whole life in humility, whereas if your own efforts were crowned by success you would not get any compassion from Jesus. He would let you climb up all by yourself and he would have to fear all the time lest you fall, because of your self-complacency."*[38]

The child presents herself before God with "empty hands." That is why she does not fear the judgment of God:

"If you don't want to ever fear again," Thérèse said to me one day, *"do as I do: take the means to force God not to judge you at all, by presenting yourself to him with empty hands. This means, don't hold onto anything for yourself, give all your merits to souls as you acquire them; in that way God can't judge something that is no longer yours!"*

"But if God doesn't judge my good deeds, he will judge my bad ones!"

"What are you saying! Our Lord, who is justice itself, can't judge

[37] CRM 84-85.

[38] CSM 49.

your bad deeds if he doesn't judge your good ones! Be assured: for the victims of Love, there will be no judgment. God will hasten to repay with eternal delights his own love that he sees burning in their heart."[39]

Note that this text wasn't used in the bishop's Process nor in the apostolic Process, whereas it was published as early as the second edition of the *Story of a Soul*.[40] Perhaps it was suggested to the witness not to add such audacious words to the dossier.

Thérèse loved the poems in which John of the Cross celebrates this fundamental value of humility. She gladly imitated with pleasure the three following lines:

> And in lowering myself so low, so low,
> I raise myself so high, so high,
> That I can reach my goal.

She was speaking of "the goal of love towards which all her desires were directed," recalled Marie of the Trinity.[41]

The Lord purifies us through even one of his glances [*ses regards*]. Thérèse loved to find this idea again in two stanzas of the *Spiritual Canticle*:

> When you gazed at me,
> Your eyes imprinted upon me their grace;
> This is why you have loved me with tenderness.
> With this grace my eyes were able
> To adore what they saw in you.
> Do not wish to despise me
> Because, if before, you found my skin dark,
> Now you can see me well,

---

[39] CRM 51-53.
[40] HA 99, p. 270 f.
[41] CSM 31.

Since you have left grace and beauty in me
By setting your eyes upon me.[42]

Thérèse never ceased denouncing the demon of selfish
pride:

*"He turns endlessly around us. It is so easy to blind oneself, to
wrap oneself in darkness... Look at poor Lamennais[43] who had nevertheless written such beautiful things about humility! Everything that
one can say and write is nothing. What has to be preserved is the disposition at each moment to accept humbly to be reproved, even if one
is not aware of having been wrong and, above all, not to excuse oneself interiorly. The humble peace that results will be the reward of our
effort. It is good for us and even necessary to see ourselves sometimes
humiliated, in order to confirm our imperfection; that is much better
for us than rejoicing about our progress. In order to help yourself, repeat with trust this prayer, especially in the moment of struggle: 'Jesus,
sweet and humble of heart, make my heart like yours.' Soon after, you
will feel the quenching of pride and the strength of practicing humility."[44]*

Thérèse took advantage of the least little occasion to form
her novices in humility. One feast day, Marie of the Trinity

---

[42] CSM 31. These stanzas 23-24 differ somewhat in Spanish from the French
version cited by the author. For example, the French uses the formal *vous*
whereas John of the Cross uses the Spanish personal *tú*, the French *tu*. The
phrase *vous m'aimiez avec tendresse* ("you have loved me with tenderness") is *me
adamabas* in Spanish ("you have ravished me with love" or "you have loved me
passionately"). In this commentary on the Song of Songs, the reference to dark
skin comes from 1:5-6, "I am black but beautiful.... Do not gaze at me because I
am swarthy, because the sun has scorched me." The dark color is not deroga-
tory, but an image to represent obscurity: the person can't be seen because she
is not what she is created to be, she is without God, without grace, not herself,
"in the dark." This is why she fears that the Beloved may despise her or at least
have trouble seeing her. But now she is confident that the presence of the
Beloved's love and grace within her make her entirely visible to him as her best
self, with God, enabled to love him with his own love (trans.).

[43] Felicité de Lamennais (1782-1854) was a liberal priest who left the Church after
his political ideas were condemned by Pope Gregory XVI.

[44] CRM 86 bis.

didn't get her share of dessert. After dinner when she was visiting the infirmary, she adroitly let her refectory neighbor know that she had been forgotten. Halting the conversation, Thérèse obliged the novice to go and notify the Sister in charge of the serving. Marie of the Trinity begged Thérèse not to impose such a step on her, but to let it go at that:

> *"This will be your penance! You are not worthy of the sacrifices that God asked of you. He asked you to be deprived of your dessert, because it is he who has permitted you to be forgotten. He thought you were sufficiently generous for this sacrifice, and you cheated his expectation by craving to have it."*[45]

The desire to please and to be loved is quite natural. But it will never be completely satisfied except in heaven:

> "Why do you want so much to be ignored and counted for nothing? As for me, I find it very pleasant to be loved and recognized."

> *"I am very much of the same opinion,"* answered Thérèse. *"It is precisely because I thirst for love and glory that I despise those of earth, which are nothing but mirages and illusions. Only in heaven can I enjoy them truly and fully. There, for me to be satisfied, I need the love of every heart, and if there were even only one missing, it would seem that I couldn't prevent myself from saying to Jesus, like Haman about Mordecai: 'Lord, as long as this one doesn't love me, my happiness will not be complete!'"*[46]

Anyway, true beauty is interior:

> *"The true, the only beauty is holiness: there is no other! A vir-*

---

[45] CRM 48-49.

[46] CRM 86-87. The reference to Haman is an example of Thérèse's amazing and audacious creativity, "inverting" a story of hatred, given in Esther 3, into an application regarding love: "And all the king's servants... bowed down and prostrated themselves before Haman... But Mordecai did not bow down or prostrate himself... And when Haman saw that Mordecai did not bow down or prostrate himself before him, Haman was filled with fury" (trans.).

tuous person, however ugly she might be, has a charm one can't resist; a person with looks but without virtue is as disagreeable as can be!"[47]

The temptations of selfish pride are more dangerous than those of impurity. One day Thérèse explained what she meant when the young Sister was complaining of scruples on this subject:

"It is amazing how easily souls lose peace when it comes to this virtue of purity! The devil is well aware of this: that is why he torments them so much on this subject. However, there is no temptation less dangerous than that one. The means of being freed from these temptations is to regard them with calm, not to be astonished, much less, to fear them. Normally with the first occurrence, one is terrified, one believes everything is lost. It is exactly this fear, this discouragement of which the devil takes advantage in order to make souls fall. However, be sure that one temptation of pride is by far more dangerous — and God is much more offended when we yield to that — than when one commits a fault, even a grave one, against purity, because God has consideration for the fragility of our corruptible nature, whereas for a fault of pride there is no excuse. Pride, however, is a fault that souls commit often and easily, without being upset! A fault of pride should be feared more than fire, whereas a temptation against purity can only humiliate our soul and by humiliation do more good than evil."[48]

Besides, temptations contribute to the purification of our soul, when we resist them:

"Keep in mind the method used to make copper objects shine. You smear them all over with mud, with things that make them dirty and dull; after this operation, they will shine again like gold. Okay! Temptations are like this mud for the soul: they serve for nothing less

---

[47] CSM 54.
[48] CRM 49-51.

*than to make the virtues which are opposed to these same temptations
to shine forth."*[49]

Let us be particularly on our guard after a retreat. But on
the other hand, let's not be discouraged because we lose the first
skirmishes. One day when Marie of the Trinity confided in
Thérèse the fervor of being loved that she felt at the end of a
retreat, Thérèse said to her:

*"Watch yourself! I have always noticed that hell is loosed against
a soul who has just finished a retreat. The demons get together to make
us fall as soon as we take the first steps, in order to discourage us. In
fact, once fallen we say: 'How can I hold on to my resolutions since,
as of this moment, I have lost them?' When we reason like that, the
demons are already the victors. It is necessary then, that each time they
throw you down, you pick yourself up without surprise and humbly
say to Jesus: 'Even though he has just now made me fall, I'm not conquered. Here I am again at the beginning, ready to recommence the
fight for love of you.' Jesus, who is touched by your good will, will
himself be your strength."*[50]

AN AUDACIOUS CONFIDENCE

Our confidence in God must be as radical as our mistrust of
ourselves. Thérèse loved to repeat with John of the Cross that
"one obtains from God as much as one hopes for."

She said that she felt infinite desires within her to love
God, to glorify him and to make him loved and that she
firmly hoped that her desires will all become reality in
heaven! She said it would be a disregard of the almighty
power and infinite goodness of God to restrain our desires and hopes but, to the contrary, it would glorify him
to nurture and increase them within ourselves.

---

[49] CRM 51.
[50] CRM 45-46.

"People would think me out of my mind if I were to enumerate all that I desire from God. My infinite desires are my riches and, for me, they fulfill the word of Jesus: 'To the one who has will more be given in abundance' (Mt 25:29). 'Good measure, pressed down and overflowing, will be put into your lap' (Lk 6:38)."[51]

A word from Job enthuses her. A word that she discovered in a prize-book,[52] perhaps around the age of 11: "Even though he should slay me, I would still hope in him" (Job 13:15). Yes, when all seems lost, it is the moment to hope against all hope. Making an allusion to her own night of faith, Thérèse confided to her novice one day:

"God will grow weary of testing me before I would ever doubt him. Even though he should slay me, I would still hope in him."[53]

We remember how many difficulties Marie of the Trinity had encountered when she entered the Carmel of Lisieux.

"Do you have confidence that you will be successful anyway?" Thérèse asked her one day.

— "Yes, I am so convinced that God will give me this grace that nothing can make me doubt it."

— *"Hold on tight to your confidence,"* answered Thérèse. *"It is impossible for God not to respond to that, because he always measures his gifts by how much confidence we have."*[54]

Even our sins must not prevail upon our confidence. Also, we mustn't wait until we are perfect to offer ourselves to the invasion of merciful Love. On November 30, 1895, the evening before she pronounced her Act of Offering, Marie of the Trin-

---

[51] CRM 16-17.

[52] *The Theology of Plants* or *The Intimate History of the World of Plants*, by l'abbé Chaudé (BT, p. 17).

[53] CRM 17.

[54] CRM 18-19.

ity felt terribly unworthy to go through with this step. Thérèse explained to her:

> "Yes, this Act is even more important than we can imagine. But do you know what God requires of us by way of preparation? He requires us to admit our unworthiness. Since he has already given you this grace, give yourself up to him without fear. Tomorrow morning after the thanksgiving, I will stay close to you in the oratory and while you make your Act, I will offer you to Jesus as the little victim that I have prepared for him."[55]

We shouldn't deprive ourselves of Holy Communion on the grounds that we have committed some sin of weakness. One day the novice wrote to Thérèse that, to punish herself for some fault, she had decided to deprive herself of Communion the next day. Thérèse told her immediately that she should, on the contrary, let herself be strengthened by the Eucharist, like the forget-me-not that half-opens its corolla to the dewdrops.[56]

Besides, we can also ask Our Lady herself to prepare us to receive the Sacrament, since we feel we are "too poor in love." Without knowing it, Thérèse here took up the method dear to Louis-Marie Grignion de Montfort.[57] The childlike images would have been happily familiar to the author of the *Treatise on True Devotion to the Blessed Virgin*:

> "At the moment of receiving Communion," Thérèse explained, "I sometimes imagine my soul being in the body of a three- or four-year-old child who, while she was playing, gets her hair messed up and her clothes dirty and disheveled. These misfortunes have happened to me because I was doing battle with souls. But immediately the Virgin Mary is there to take charge of me: she quickly rearranges my dirty apron, fixes my hair and puts a nice ribbon in it, or simply a little flower

---

[55] CSM 38.

[56] LT 240.

[57] *On True Devotion*, °266. See A 79 v - 80 r.

... and that's enough to make me graceful and able to partake in the banquet of the angels without embarrassment."[58]

Thérèse also made proof of this audacious hope in her responsibility towards the novitiate. When she did not make herself understood to Marie of the Trinity, Thérèse asked the Lord to himself enlighten the heart of this very young sister. During the winter of 1895-1896, there came an evening when Marie of the Trinity did have this happy experience. After a whole day of doing laundry she went to Thérèse, tired and discouraged.

"The bell is ringing for prayer," Thérèse responded, *"I have no time to console you. Besides, I see clearly that I would be wasting my time; God wants you to suffer alone for the moment."*

The novice took herself to choir to participate in the prayer, but in such a battered state that, for the first time, she seriously doubted her vocation. Outside, there was a storm: the wind howled and rattled the choir windows; inside, there was anguish:

> "I will never have the strength to be a Carmelite," I said to myself; "it's too hard a life for me!"
> I had been kneeling for several minutes in this state of agitation and sad thoughts when, all of a sudden, without having prayed or even yearned for peace, I felt an extraordinary change in my soul. I didn't recognize myself anymore. My vocation seemed to me beautiful, loveable; I had seen the value of suffering. All the privations and the fatigues of religious life seemed to me infinitely more desirable than mundane satisfactions. I left prayer absolutely transformed.
> After supper I happily proposed to myself to wash dishes; I did not think of my headache anymore, I wanted to start another laundry day with a good heart in order to suffer more.

---

[58] CRM 20.

The next morning I told Sr. Thérèse of the Child Jesus what had happened the night before and, since she seemed quite moved, I wanted to know why.

"Ah!" she said to me, *"How good God is! Last night I felt such a profound pity for you that, from the beginning of prayer, I didn't cease praying for you, asking Our Lord to console you, to bring about a change in your soul and to show you the value of suffering. He heard me!"*

"While saying these words, she shed tears and I cried myself, from joy and gratitude."[59]

TO DO EVERYTHING OUT OF LOVE

Our confidence in the Lord's mercy must not be a pretext to try to live an easy life. His generosity and his desire to give love for love are essential to the way of confidence AND love. One day when Marie of the Trinity shared with Thérèse her intention to explain the "Little Way" to her parents, Thérèse cautioned her:

"Be very careful how you explain it, because our 'Little Way' badly understood could be taken for quietism or illuminism."

And Thérèse told her about the errors of Mme. Guyon.[60]

"Don't think," she continued, *"that to follow the path of love means to follow the path of repose, full of sweetness and consolations. It is completely the opposite. To offer oneself as a victim to Love means to give oneself up without any reservations to whatever God pleases, which means to expect to share with Jesus his humiliations, his chalice of bitterness."*[61]

---

[59] CSM 1.

[60] Mme. Guyon (1648-1717) promoted the error of Quietism, which taught that the soul should be completely passive in relation to God.

[61] CRM 26-27.

Without having made a vow of being or doing what was "most perfect," Thérèse insisted on refusing nothing to God. Questioned on this subject by her companion, she answered:

"It isn't necessary to have made such a vow in order to really live it. As for me, I always insist on acting as if I had made a vow. Besides, I can't understand how a soul who loves God, and above all a Carmelite, could act otherwise because it is an obligation of our vocation."[62]

The mediocrity of the community in which we live is never a valid excuse for personal slackness:

"When everyone fails to follow the Rule," she said, *"it isn't a reason to justify ourselves; everyone must act as if the regularity and the perfection of the Order pertain only to our own personal conduct."*[63]

Marie of the Trinity underlined the heroism with which Thérèse lived this fidelity under Mother Marie de Gonzague's term as prioress.[64]

Nothing is small in the life of a Carmelite, not even the care with which one makes one's bed.[65] The important thing is to do everything out of love.

In 1894, Thérèse was very happy to come upon the following exhortation — an excerpt from the retreat led by P. Boulanger at the Paris Carmel:

If, at each moment, he would ask you: "What are you doing?" your response should be: "I love!"
"In the refectory?" — "I love!"
"In choir?" — "I love!"
"Anywhere?" — "I love!"

Thérèse carefully kept this note.

---

[62] CRM 2-3.
[63] CRM 3.
[64] CRM 2.
[65] CRM 4.

"It is," she said, *"the echo of my soul. For a long time this is how I have understood love and how I have exerted myself to practice it!"*[66]

That all her actions might become acts of love, Thérèse wanted to be hypnotized, or "magnetized" by Jesus. One day, her companion had told her about some hypnotism experiments in which some of the girls from her boarding school, St. Geneviève d'Asnières, had taken part. The next day, Thérèse said to her:

"Your conversation yesterday did me so much good! Oh! how much I would like to be magnetized by our Lord! This was the first thought that came to me when I woke up. How sweetly I would surrender my will to him. Yes, I would like him to take possession of all my faculties in such a way that I would no longer perform actions that are human and personal, but only divine actions, inspired and directed by the Spirit of love."[67]

As Elisha had asked to receive the double spirit of Elijah [cf. 2 Kings 2:9], Thérèse implored the saints to obtain for her their double love. In return, she gave over to them all the glory that they would help her to acquire. Her favorite saints? St. Joseph, the Holy Innocents, St. Cecilia, Théophane Vénard, Joan of Arc. She liked to praise the special virtues of each one, to encourage her youngest novice to imitate them.[68]

The eagerness to work is just as important as the regularity of the life of prayer. One day when the novice asked to be

---

[66] CRM 23-24.

[67] CSM 11. Hypnotism was still sometimes referred to as "animal magnetism," and was a very popular subject at the time. See, for example, in *Le Normand*, the publicity caused by the celebrated Pickman, "magnetist, medium, reader of thoughts, hypnotist," September 17, 1895. It is not immediately clear what distinction, if any, is implied here between "magnetist" and "hypnotist." A good idea of popular contemporary ideas on hypnotism can be found in George du Maurier's 1894 novel, *Trilby*, which featured the hypnotist Svengali.

[68] CRM 14-15.

excused from an hour of prayer in order to finish an urgent task, Thérèse said to her:

"Unless it is for a great necessity, never ask permission to miss the community exercises for any work whatsoever; this dedication can't be pleasing to Jesus. Real dedication is never to lose a minute and to give oneself fully during the hours designated for work."[69]

The recitation of the Divine Office should be animated by the fundamental desire to please God. Thérèse often urged the novices not to neglect the "little means" that facilitate putting oneself in the Lord's presence. She herself had an irreproachable bearing during prayer:

"If you were having an audience at the court of an earthly king," she said to me, *"your dress and your bearing would be impeccable, each of your movements would be studied. How much more must you behave correctly in the presence of the King of kings and of the heavenly court that forms his entourage? To refrain — because of the divine presence — from moving, from touching your face or clothing, gives the greatest pleasure to God because he sees how much we esteem him and love him."*[70]

Thérèse was pleased to find this primacy of love expressed in certain passages of John of the Cross that she cited most gladly. Mainly these:

"It is of the greatest importance that the soul exercise itself constantly in love so that, consuming itself rapidly, it hardly stops here on earth and arrives promptly in seeing God face to face.

"In the evening of this life, you will be judged on love. Learn therefore to love God as he ought to be loved and forget yourself."[71]

---

[69] CRM 46-47.
[70] CRM 11-12.
[71] CRM 24. See LT 245; DE, p. 492 f.; LT 188.

"*He is the saint of love par excellence,*" Thérèse said of St. John of the Cross.[72]

Love in no way relegates the other evangelical virtues to the background. Thérèse explained this one day to Marie of the Trinity, from one of the verses of the Song of Songs: "We shall make for you chains of gold inlaid with silver" (1:10).

"*What a strange thing to say! It would be more understandable if the spouse said to his beloved: we shall make you silver chains inlaid with gold or gold chains inlaid with precious stones, because normally you don't enhance a precious jewel with an inferior metal. During my prayer, Jesus gave me the key to the mystery. I understood that the gold chains stand for love, for charity, and that they can't be pleasing to Jesus unless they are inlaid with silver, which means humility, simplicity and a childlike spirit. Oh! who can tell what value God attributes to these humble virtues, since they alone are found worthy to enhance the luster of charity.*"[73]

TO PLEASE GOD

Thérèse was so happy to be able to give pleasure to God that she sought no other reward. This made her embarrassed by a psalm verse they recited every morning during prayer: "*Inclinávi cor meum ad faciéndas iustificatiónes tuas in æternum, propter retributiónem,*" which means: "I have set my heart on keeping your commandments always because of the reward" (Psalm 118:112).

"*Within myself,*" she confided, "*I hastened to say: 'Oh Jesus, you know very well that I don't serve you for the reward, but solely because I love you and to save souls.'*"[74] But she was "reconciled"

---

[72] CRM 31.
[73] CRM 10-11.
[74] CRM 30.

with that verse when she was reminded of the word of John of the Cross: "The soul who loves God must not want or hope for any other reward for her services than the perfection of divine love."[75] But mainly Thérèse would have appreciated the translation of the new Jerusalem Bible: "Bending my heart to do your will is my reward forever," or the one of the T.O.B.[76]: "To apply myself to practicing your decrees is forever my reward."

For the same reason her faithfulness at every moment did not have a fear of purgatory as its motive, but rather the desire to "give love" to her God:

"If I were unfaithful, I wouldn't go straight to heaven, would I?" Marie of the Trinity asked one day.

"Oh, that isn't how it is!" answered Thérèse. *"God is so good that he would arrange it in such a way that you wouldn't lose anything; he is the one who would lose love!"*[77]

Thérèse's desire to suffer would be incomprehensible without this sensitivity, without this incessant desire to prove her love to the Beloved. One day, when Marie of the Trinity confided to Thérèse her fear of suffering, the novice understood her to reply:

"Oh! nothing can be too much for me! Here on earth I love to suffer more rather than less!"

— "But why?"

— *"Ah, because we have only this one lifetime in which to prove our love!"*[78]

---

[75] *Spiritual Canticle*, stanza 9.

[76] *Traduction d'Oecuménique de la Bible* (trans.).

[77] CRM 32.

[78] CRM 45.

THE REWARD OF SUFFERING

John of the Cross had taught Thérèse the reward of suffering. In order to arrive at the perfect union of love, one must accept to pass through the crucible of trial. She would recite from memory the passages where he himself had been comforted in his tribulations and in his night of faith:

> "O souls who seek to live in joy and security, if you only knew how good it is for you to be afflicted in order to arrive at that state where you would never look for consolation anymore, you would want nothing other than the cross with its gall and bitterness, you would regard yourself as supremely happy to have a share in it.… In suffering outward trials patiently, you would become worthy for the Lord to set his divine eyes [*regards*] upon you and purify you by interior, more intimate sufferings."

Thérèse added: *"When we truly welcome suffering, we merit the grace of a much greater suffering or, rather, of a much deeper purification, in order to arrive at the perfect union of love. When I had understood that, strength was given to me to suffer everything."*[79]

On the occasion when Marie of the Trinity took the veil, Thérèse offered her an image of John of the Cross. On the front she had written the exclamation that she had often meditated upon at *Les Buissonnets*, when she was around fifteen: "To suffer and to be despised for love!"[80] On the back, she had copied three of the saint's thoughts. Two of them reminded her pre-

---

[79] CSM 31. *The Living Flame of Love*, explication of the 2nd stanza, v. 5. Testimony of 1926. In 1942, Marie of the Trinity again quoted the text of John of the Cross, adding: "It is, above all, a passage from *The Living Flame of Love* that wondrously strengthened her during the time of her great sufferings: '*I found it so uplifting and profound*,' she told me, '*that when reading it I am like someone infatuated: it takes my breath away.*'"

[80] CSM 31.

cisely of the fact that you can't have real love without renunciation: "The one who truly loves God seeks no other goal and reward than to lose everything and to lose even oneself for God." — "In the evening of this life, we will be judged on love. Learn then to love God as he desires to be loved and forget about yourself."[81]

Among the sentences from the *Ascent of Mount Carmel* that Marie of the Trinity had copied for the feast of John of the Cross in November 1895, Thérèse particularly appreciated these: "There is no path through here because there is no law for the just." — "Everything is being given to me without my looking for it, since I did not desire anything from a motive of vanity."[82]

Thérèse had never lost the desire of martyrdom, which lived in her ever since she knelt in the Coliseum and the catacombs of St. Callixtus in Rome. During the whole of 1894, while she was preparing her second play about Joan of Arc, this desire for martyrdom only grew deeper and more profound. This same year, 1894, was the centennial celebration for the sixteen Carmelite martyrs of Compiègne who were beheaded during the Revolution. When Thérèse heard the prioress telling stories about how the government was again increasingly harassing religious communities, she responded happily:

"What a joy! God is going to make the most beautiful dream of my life come true! We are living in an age of martyrs! ... Let's not suffer anymore from the little miseries of life; let's live them generously in order to become worthy of so great a grace."[83]

In any case, our acts of love are pretty small compared to the "follies" that the Lord undertook for us and that he rightfully expects on our part, too. One day, when her disciple was boasting about some virtuous act that she had just done, Thérèse retorted:

---

[81] *Spiritual thoughts and recommendations*, sentences 103 and 70.
[82] CSM 31.
[83] CRM 61-62.

"What is so amazing about how you have acted? When you think of all the lights and all the graces that Jesus gives you, you would have been pretty guilty to have acted otherwise. What is that compared to what he has the right to expect from your faithfulness? You should rather be humbling yourself for letting so many opportunities go by for practicing virtue!"[84]

A HEROIC LOVE

Love must above all express itself through fidelity at every moment. Marie of the Trinity had been a privileged witness of the heroism with which Thérèse put her will to work never to refuse anything to God.

Mortifications of the body

Although she sat next to her in the refectory, the novice could never catch a clue about what Thérèse liked or didn't like: she ate everything without giving the impression of preferring one thing to another. When she became very ill and the infirmarian obliged her to say what she could eat, she had to admit that certain foods always made her sick.

Thérèse herself was the first to observe the advice that she gave to others concerning mortification: never lean against the wall while you eat, don't mix the food on your plate in order to make it taste better, end your meal with a small piece of dry bread.

"All these little nothings," she said, *"don't jeopardize the health, they don't attract people's attention, they keep our soul spiritually alert and zealous for what pertains to God."*

---

[84] CRM 47-48.

In order to mitigate the Lenten fast for the sick Thérèse in 1897, Mother Marie de Gonzague made her eat a very small piece of chocolate each morning. But to temper this sweet, Thérèse also put a little piece of bitter wood in her mouth.

> She hid this mortification carefully: only with skill did I manage to discover it.
> For her personally, the cold was the most painful corporal mortification that she endured in Carmel, but she bore it so heroically without ever complaining or looking for relief. She reproved me when I was showing how cold I was by being huddled up or shivering. One day I hung my slippers on a heater to dry. Noticing that, Thérèse said to me:

> *"If I had done what you just did, I would have thought I was committing a grave fault against mortification. But what is the point of embracing an austere way of life, if we only seek to relieve ourselves of everything that could make us suffer? Without an order under obedience, we shouldn't avoid even the smallest practice of mortification."*[85]

A heroic obedience

Thérèse wanted to do nothing unless she had explicit permission for it:

> *"These little subjugations make us practice our vow of obedience to perfection. If we try to avoid them, what good does it do us to have made this vow?"*

She was especially admirable in the way she submitted herself to "the multitude of petty rules that Mother Marie de Gonzague established or abolished at the whim of her caprices" — rules that most of the Sisters didn't observe at all. Thérèse

---

[85] CRM 69-71.

also obeyed with the same readiness the wishes of all the Sisters in the community.

> At the first sound of the bell she interrupted her work. She was extremely vigilant not to talk to me during the great silence: there was not even an urgent matter of charity that could make her break this rule.

In order to encourage Marie of the Trinity to obedience, Thérèse confided to her the act of submission that was imposed on her at the beginning of her religious life:

"Sr. Marie of the Angels, our mistress of novices, ordered me to tell her each time I had a stomach ache. Since this happened to me every day, this order became a real torture for me. When the stomach ache started, I would have preferred one hundred blows of the stick rather than go and tell her, but out of obedience I did go each time. Sr. Marie of the Angels — who often didn't remember what she had commanded — said to me: 'Poor child, you will never be healthy enough to observe the Rule, it is too hard for you!' Or else, she would ask Mother Marie de Gonzague for some medicine for me, who answered rather annoyed: 'Really! this child is always complaining! We come to Carmel to suffer! If she can't bear her illness, she should leave!' Nevertheless, out of obedience I continued to report my stomach aches for quite a while, at the risk of being sent away, until God took pity on my weakness by permitting them to release me from the obligation of having to do so."[86]

A perfect chastity

At the age of fourteen Thérèse was finally freed from a crisis of scruples that she had suffered for eighteen months. Now she could live her vow of chastity in great peace. Everything about her breathed of purity, the former novice testified. More-

---

[86] CRM 72-76.

over, she learned to look upon every creature with a luminous regard:

"Everything is pure for the pure," she would often say to me; *"the bad exists only in a perverse will."*

Also by her bearing, Thérèse reminded herself that she was always in the presence of God:

"When I am alone, whether it be when I get up or go to bed, I always am extremely careful to be as modest as I would if other people were present. After all, am I not always in the presence of God and his angels? This modesty has become such a habit for me that I wouldn't know how to act otherwise."[87]

An authentic poverty

Thérèse also cared a lot about not wasting anything.

She kept the wick of her oil lamp very short in order to receive only the minimum amount of light. She mended her clothes as long as possible in order to avoid buying new ones. With that same sense of poverty she always wrote her lines very close together in order to use less paper.[88]

She would assure me that it was very desirable to lack necessary things, because then you could call yourself truly poor. She told me that for shopping, I should unhesitatingly buy the least expensive things in order to be and do like the poor.[89]

---

[87] CRM 77-78.

[88] CRM 76-77.

[89] CRM 77.

Jérusalem
Carmel du Pater Noster

FLEURS DU MONT DES OLIVIERS
BÉNITES SUR LE ST-SÉPULCRE.

Holy cards with an image of
Jesus, the cross and the crib
given to Thérèse by Sr.
Marie of the Trinity on the
day of Marie's profession,
April 30. 1896.

Fleurs de ✠ Bethléem

Posées sur l'autel de la Crèche
de N. S. J. C.

LA SAINTE FACE DE NOTRE SEIGNEUR

Card showing the Holy Face of Our Lord, for Marie-Louise Castel's Taking of the Habit in the Parisian Carmel of l'avenue Messine, May 12, 1892.

Mr. and Mrs. Castel have the honor to inform you that on Thursday, May 12, at 2:00 in the afternoon, the solemn ceremony of the Clothing of their daughter Marie-Louise Castel, known in religion as Sister Agnes of Jesus will take place at the Carmel at 23 l'avenue Messine.

Prayers of good will are welcomed.

« INVITATION ❖ ET ❖ SOUVENIR »

Monsieur et Madame CASTEL ont l'honneur de vous informer que le Jeudi 12 Mai, à 2 heures de l'après-midi, aura lieu au Carmel de l'Avenue de Messine, 23, la cérémonie solennelle de la Vêture de leur fille Marie-Louise Castel, en religion Sœur AGNÈS DE JÉSUS.

Prière de bien vouloir y assister.

First Communion card of Marguerite-Marie Castel, younger sister of Marie of the Trinity, Providence Convent of Lisieux, May 24, 1894.

Icon of Our Lady of Perpetual Help, like the one kept in the oratory of Marie's childhood home.

Poem offered by Thérèse to Sr. Marie of the Trinity on the occasion of her profession on April 30, 1896.

Holy card given by Thérèse to Sr. Marie of the Trinity on the occasion of her taking of the Veil, May 7, 1896. Thérèse has used a photograph of a painting of St. John of the Cross done by Mother Agnes.

Sr. Marie of the Trinity made herself this picture of the Holy Family for her breviary, resembling the one of Thérèse, for her own 23rd birthday. She copied the same text and asked for a last dedication from Thérèse, who was to die six weeks later.

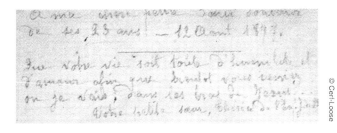

Levez les yeux et voyez comme les campagnes sont déjà assez blanches pour être moissonnées...

(St. Jean IV. 35.)

La moisson est grande, mais le nombre des moissonneurs est petit, priez donc le Maître de la moisson qu'Il envoie des moissonneurs...... L'un sème et l'autre moissonne... et celui qui sème se réjouira comme celui qui moissonne.... Je suis venu apporter le feu sur la terre et qu'est-ce que je désire sinon qu'on l'allume?.....

Matt. IX — Jean. IV — Luc. XII. 49

"To my dear little Sister in remembrance of her 23rd birthday. May your life be all humility and love, that you may soon come to where I am going: in the arms of Jesus.... Your little sister, Thérèse of the Child Jesus of the Holy Face."

Card composed by Sr. Marie of the Trinity after Thérèse's death.

Fr. Daniel Brottier, administrator of the Orphans-Apprentices of Auteil, who asked Marie to become the spiritual godmother of this Work.

PHOT. BOIVIN

LE PÈRE
DANIEL BROTTIER

Assistant Général des Pères du Saint-Esprit, Directeur de l'Œuvre des Orphelins-Apprentis d'Auteuil, Missionnaire au Sénégal, Fondateur du Souvenir Africain, Officier de la Légion d'honneur, Croix de Guerre, décédé saintement, le 28 février 1936, à l'âge de 59 ans.

ÉTOFFE AYANT TOUCHÉ AU PÈRE BROTTIER

Holy card of the Presentation of Mary offered to Thérèse on the day of her profession, by Sister Agnes [Pauline] and Sr. Marie of the Sacred Heart [Marie].

Thérèse and her youngest novice, Sr. Marie of the Trinity and of the Holy Face, taken on March 17, 1896, six weeks before Marie's profession (April 30).

© Ceri-Loose

Photograph taken on April 30, 1896, the profession of Sr. Marie of the Trinity.

The three who made the Act of Consecration to the Holy Face,
composed by Thérèse. The photos were taken around July 3, 1896.
Thérèse arranged them around the picture of the Holy Face.

Thérèse and Marie.

The Novitiate celebrating the
feast of the Good Shepherd,
Sunday, April 28, 1895.

Another view of the Novitiate celebrating the feast of the Good Shepherd,
Sunday, April 28, 1895.

Community recreation.

Community recreation some time after the death of Thérèse in the Carmel of Lisieux.

Statue of St. Thérèse marking the grave of Sr. Marie of the Trinity and her companions in the Carmelite section of the Lisieux cemetery.

Reverse side of the statue: names of Sr. Martha of Jesus, Sr. Marie
Madeleine of the Blessed Sacrament and
Sr. Marie of the Trinity.

Group photograph (April 15, 1895)

1. Sr. Thérèse of the Child Jesus
2. Sr. Marie of the Sacred Heart (Marie)
3. Reverend Mother Agnes of Jesus (Pauline)
4. Sr. Geneviève of the Holy Face (Céline)
5. Sr. Marie of the Eucharist (Marie Guérin)
6. Reverend Mother Marie de Gonzague

In the order of profession

7. Sr. Saint Stanislaus
8. Mother Hermance of the Sacred Heart of Jesus
9. Sr. Marie of the Angels
10. Sr. Saint Raphael
11. Sr. Saint John the Baptist
12. Sr. Aimée of Jesus
13. Sr. Thérèse of Jesus
14. Sr. Marguerite Marie
15. Sr. Thérèse of Saint Augustine
16. Sr. Saint John of the Cross
17. Sr. Marie Emmanuel
18. Sr. Marie of Saint Joseph
19. Sr. Marie of Jesus
20. Sr. Marie Philomène
21. Sr. Marie of the Trinity
22. Sr. Anne of the Sacred Heart (from the Carmel of Saigon)

Extern Sisters ("Converses")

23. Sr. Marie of the Incarnation
24. Sr. Saint Vincent de Paul
25. Sr. Martha of Jesus
26. Sr. Marie Madeleine

Mother Agnes of Jesus, holding a sheaf; Sr. Marie of the Trinity is on the far right. The picture was taken in 1919, four years before Sr. Marie of the Trinity, age 35, contracted lupus.

Faithfulness in little things

Thérèse knew that it is better to have great fidelity in little things than to have little fidelity in big things. She herself was the first to abide by the rules of Carmel that she explained to the novitiate:

> When I wanted to remember the text of our rules, all I had to do was watch what Thérèse did.[90]

Thérèse thus prepared herself to bear heroically the suffering of her tuberculosis: several hours after her first hemoptysis (spitting up of blood), the morning of Good Friday 1896, she shared with Marie of the Trinity, now assistant infirmarian, what had happened to her:

> Her face was shining with happiness in the hope of soon going to see God; she also expressed her joy to me about what Mother Marie de Gonzague had so easily permitted her: to take part in all the penitential exercises of the last two days of Holy Week, despite this incident. She made me promise to keep secret this sad news (which she called happy!), so as not to distress Mother Agnes. I thus kept for myself alone the weight of this immense pain, which was increased by an inner revolt against the imprudence of Mother Marie de Gonzague who, not only let her nurse herself, but risked increasing her illness by her insane permission.
>
> So, this Good Friday she fasted the whole day like all of us, not eating more than a little dry bread and drinking only water, at noon and at 6 p.m. On top of it, in between the hours of prayer, she didn't stop doing very fatiguing house cleaning. In the afternoon I saw her climb a ladder to wash the window panes and, shocked by her pale and exhausted face, I begged her in tears to

---

[90] CRM 56.

let me help her finish her work. But she refused, telling me that she could easily bear a slight fatigue on this day when Jesus had suffered so much for her. In the evening she again took the discipline. Then when she returned exhausted to her cell, she was taken again by the same spitting up of blood as the evening before.[91]

This same heroic conduct continued in the following months. She followed all of the community exercises and maintained her smile. She admitted that, often during the recitation of the Office, she couldn't hold herself upright without doing violence to herself and that she helped alleviate her tiredness by remembering the words of the soldier on the battlefield who went out to seize the enemy flag crying: *"When I die, everybody will clearly see it!"*

When I realized that she was at the end of her strength, I went to Mother Marie de Gonzague to ask to have her dispensed from at least the office of Matins, but my intervention was completely in vain. She told me: "How come young people like you pay attention to your smallest weaknesses and seek to be dispensed from the fatigues of the Rule! In former times, no one ever missed Matins! If Sr. Thérèse of the Child Jesus can no longer do it, she can come and tell me so herself!" But Thérèse never went to complain and when she learned that I had gone for her, she begged me not to go anymore. She assured me that Mother Prioress was aware of her tiredness and that she was inspired by God, who wanted to grant her desire to go to the very end of her strength, without any relief.[92]

During her illness, Thérèse had as a principle to never ask for anything. This is reported by the same witness:

---

[91] CRM 64-65.
[92] CRM 65-66.

"One evening the infirmarian came to put a hot water bottle at my feet and a tincture of iodine on my chest. I was already consumed by fever, a burning thirst devoured me. In undergoing these remedies, I could not help complaining to our Lord: 'My Jesus, you are my witness: I am already boiling and they bring me more heat and more fire! Ah! If only I had half a glass of water instead!… My Jesus! Your little girl is really thirsty! But she is glad, anyway, to find the opportunity to lack what she needs, so as to resemble you more and save souls.' Soon the infirmarian left me and I didn't expect to see her until the next morning, when to my great surprise she returned a few minutes later with a refreshing drink…. Oh! how good our Jesus is! It is so easy to entrust ourselves to him!"[93]

This abandonment to the good pleasure of God, such as it manifests itself through human beings, is something Thérèse had lived for a long time:

"When you are sick," she told me, *"say so quite simply to Mother Prioress, then give yourself over to God, without troubling whether they take care of you or not. You have done your part by saying it: that is sufficient. The rest is not for you to look after: it is God's concern. When he lets you lack something, this is a grace; it is because he has confidence that you are strong enough to suffer something for him."*[94]

THE JOY OF SAVING SOULS

Thérèse was very happy to work to "earn a living" for her children, according to the expression of Sr. Marie of St. Peter, the Carmelite of Tours mentioned before.[95] She offered her life very specially for priests, gladly saying again and again that in this way she worked for the salvation of those to whom they are sent.

---

[93] CRM 21-22.
[94] CRM 20-21.
[95] CRM 28.

One day when Marie of the Trinity was sauntering along to the laundry, Thérèse overtook her.

"Is this how one hurries when one has children to feed and has to work to keep them alive?"[96]

The joy of spiritual motherhood profoundly transforms the way you look upon your work at the beginning of the day:

"Before I entered Carmel, when I woke up in the morning I used to think about what the day could possibly have in store for me, happy or troublesome, and if I foresaw only troubles, I got up depressed. Now it is the opposite. I think only of the pains and sufferings that await me, and I get up so much more joyful and full of courage when I think of the opportunities that I will have to prove my love to Jesus and earn a living for my children, since I am a mother of souls. After that I kiss my crucifix, I put it gently at my place on the pillow while I'm getting dressed, and I say to him: 'Jesus, you have worked and wept long enough during the thirty-three years of your life on this poor earth! today, you rest... It is my turn to fight and to suffer!'"[97]

Even the lack of courage became a cause for joy. One day when Marie of the Trinity was lamenting because of her lack of courage, Thérèse told her:

"You are complaining about something that should cause you the greatest happiness. Where would your merit be, if you could fight only when you feel courage? What does it matter if you have none, provided that you act as if you do! When you feel too weak to pick up a ball of yarn and you do it anyway for the love of Jesus, you have more merit than if you had accomplished something much more important in a moment of fervor. Instead of being sad when you get to feel your weakness, rejoice that God is providing you with the opportunity to save a greater number of souls for him!"[98]

---

[96] CSM 25. The "brisk step" of Thérèse allows us to situate this event in the summer of 1896.

[97] CSM 4.

[98] CRM 55.

Thérèse felt truly sorry only for those people who don't believe in the possibility of giving wondrous efficacy to their sufferings.

"The saints who suffer never make me feel pity! I know that they have the strength to bear their sufferings and that they thus give great glory to God. But those who aren't saints, who don't know how to profit from their sufferings, how I pity them! Those are the ones I really pity! I would get to work in order to console them and comfort them."[99]

This is why she suffered more from the mean jealousies to which Mother Marie de Gonzague gave free rein when Mother Agnes was prioress, than from the sufferings which resulted thereby for Mother Agnes.[100]

LOVING RELATIONSHIPS

Thérèse shared with her novices the discoveries she made in the Gospel concerning the subject of loving relationships, to which she dedicated a great part of her last manuscript:

"The principal plenary indulgence, the one that the whole world gains under common conditions," she said one day to Marie of the Trinity, *"is the indulgence of charity which covers a multitude of sins."*[101] [cf. 1 Peter 4:8.]

She possibly made this reflection in 1896, when Carmel celebrated the jubilee year accorded to France for the 14th centenary of the baptism of Clovis.

---

[99] CSM 28. According to an oral tradition, she was referring to Sr. Marie-Philomène (see *Annales*, January 1982). Thérèse expressed an opinion close to this on April 6, 1897 (DE, p. 393). But personal experience will modify her judgment. She will understand that the saints themselves can "lose patience" in suffering: *"I wouldn't have believed it before"* (CJ 8.3.4).

[100] CRM 59-60.

[101] CSM 44.

Meanwhile, it would be a mistake to think that Thérèse scorned indulgences. Here is the testimony of her former novice:

> The way of the cross had a great attraction for her soul: she loved to make the Stations as often as possible, *"as much for the good it does me personally, as to deliver souls from purgatory by this means."*[102]

An unshakable patience

Marie of the Trinity often returned to the exquisite sensitivity with which Thérèse lived her relationships in community.

During the three years of Mother Agnes' term as prioress, Thérèse was assigned to assist Sr. Saint Raphael at the turn, that is to say, to assist in the relationships with the extern Sisters (that is, the Sisters who had contact with lay people, did the shopping, etc.). Sr. Saint Raphael was a person who could "try the patience of an angel" through her numerous quirks:

> Her conversations were often just charades. She never expressed her thoughts clearly. After many detours of obscure phrases, the result was always the same: "I got you started, figure out the rest yourself!"
> One day when she was speaking to me like this, I said to her impatiently: "I'm in a hurry, tell me plainly what you want. I don't understand what you're saying."
> — "Oh, little Sister," she answered me, "Sr. Thérèse of the Child Jesus never talks to me like you do."
> When I told Thérèse about it, she confided to me:

> *"Be very gentle with her, she is sick. Besides, it's only charity to let her think that she is good for us and this gives us the opportunity to practice patience. If you are already complaining, you who have so little to do with her, what would you say if you were in my place,*

---

[102] CRM 12-13.

obliged to listen to her all day long? You can do what I do, it's not difficult. You must try not to let yourself be irritated inside and mellow your soul by loving thoughts. After that, you will practice patience as if it were natural to you."[103]

Her patience towards Sr. Marie of St. Joseph was equally remarkable. Thérèse helped her in the linen room from March 1896 to May 1897, fourteen months of difficult collaboration. Sr. Marie of St. Joseph had a violent character and Thérèse endured her very hard words without ever complaining. Through her gentleness she even managed to sometimes disarm her companion, who would then recognize her offenses herself!

Still, the fact remains that three weeks after Thérèse left her job in the linen room, she wrote in her last manuscript:

"This year, God gave me the grace to understand what charity is."[104]

The companionship of Sr. Marie of St. Joseph certainly served something very important! Now we also understand better what Thérèse meant when she wrote about "wounded souls" and the compassion one should have for their "chronic moral weaknesses."

Lastly, we know about the heroic attitude that Thérèse showed to Sr. Thérèse of St. Augustine, the Sister a little bit "stiff," whose rigidity contrasted strangely with the suppleness of Thérèse:

> She never discussed her difficulties concerning that Sister, but I was too closely united to her not to be aware of them. When I wanted to talk to her about it, she adroitly changed the conversation, which confirmed what I saw.[105]

---

[103] CRM 33-35. About Sr. Saint Raphael, see *Annales*, June 1983.

[104] CRM 35-36. About Sr. Marie of St. Joseph, see *Annales*, November 1982.

[105] CRM 38. About Sr. Thérèse of St. Augustine, see *Annales*, January 1984.

"Love does not seek its own interest"

At common work or at recreation Thérèse always sought the company of the Sisters whom she perceived to be sad and tried to help them open up by her warmth and her attentions.

"It is at recreation, more than anywhere else," she told me, *"that you find opportunities to practice virtue. If you really want to profit greatly from recreation, don't go there with the idea of having fun yourself but to help others have a good time. Practice self-detachment. For example, if you tell one of your Sisters a story that seems interesting to you and the Sister interrupts you to tell you something else, listen to her with interest, even if she doesn't interest you at all, and don't try to go back to the original conversation. If you act like this, you will come out of recreation with a great inner peace, reclothed with a new strength to practice virtue because you have not sought to satisfy yourself but to give pleasure to others. If only we knew what we gain by renouncing ourselves in everything!"*[106]

Thérèse often talked about the disinterestedness that ought to animate our relationships with others: it brings real peace.

"The main cause of your sufferings and your struggles," she said to me, *"comes from the fact that you look on things too much from an earthly point of view and not enough with the spirit of faith. You seek your own satisfactions too much. Do you know how to truly find happiness? When you don't seek it anymore. Believe me, I've experienced this."*[107]

The novice was made to remember this when she didn't follow the principle. One day when she complained about seeing Mother Agnes paying more attention to another Sister than to herself, Thérèse answered her:

"It isn't Mother Agnes you love, but yourself. When you really love, you rejoice about the happiness of the beloved person and you

---

[106] CSM 24.
[107] CRM 6.

make every sacrifice to obtain it for her. If you loved our Mother for her own sake, you would rejoice to see that she finds pleasure at your expense. Since you think that she has less pleasure talking with you than with someone else, you shouldn't be hurt because you apparently have been neglected."[108]

When Thérèse manifested her disinterested love for her novices by the severity with which she reproved them, she would say to their displeasure:

"I owe you the truth," she said to me, *"and I will tell you that until I die. I am severe, it's true, but I feel how short time is: I need to hurry up to form you to perfection because I don't have long to stay on earth.*"[109]

Spiritual friendship

Let's not now think that under the pretext of disinterestedness, Thérèse systematically deprived herself of showing her affections. Marie of the Trinity benefitted more than once from these testimonies of friendship. One day, Thérèse said to her:

"I assure you that I love you as if I had a heart for you alone!"

— "But," replied the novice, "you love your Little Mother and your other Sisters very much and it isn't possible that you love me more or even as much!"

"That can't be compared! Our heart is made in the image of God, who loves every creature as if she were the only one in the world. Likewise, the love I have for my Little Mother and my other Sisters doesn't stand in the way of the love I have for you. I have a special heart, entirely for everybody, and in spite of that, my heart belongs entirely to God. Jealousy and comparison never exist in genuine love for one's neighbor."[110]

---

[108] CRM 41-42.
[109] CRM 5-6.
[110] CSM 50.

Saying "thank you"

At the beginning of her stay in Carmel, the postulant had to come to terms with being reproached for not sufficiently showing her gratitude when she had benefitted from some service. She gave too much of an impression that she considered it her due:

"You must get used to letting your gratitude be seen, to say thank you with an open heart for the least little thing," Thérèse said. *"This is the practice of charity, to act this way; otherwise, it is indifference which, even if it is only exterior, freezes the heart and destroys the cordiality that is necessary in community."*

The witness remarks that Thérèse developed this idea in her last manuscript:

"Charity must not stay locked up at the bottom of the heart."[111]

The choice of the last place

When the community worked together, Thérèse took the most difficult part. Here again, the advice she gave shows how she did it:

"When it is hard for you to go out and rinse the linen in cold water, that means it's also hard for the others, because we all feel more or less the same thing. On the contrary, when the weather is warm, stay by preference in the laundry room to wash the linen. By taking the worst places, you at once practice mortification for yourself and charity for others, because you give up the better place to them."[112]

---

[111] C 12 r. Note to Mother Agnes, 6/13/43.
[112] CRM 36-37.

A total availability

What, according to Marie of the Trinity, had been the most visible progress that Thérèse had made, having discovered in the Gospel all the requirements of the "new commandment"?

> When she received such vivid insights concerning charity, about which she speaks in her *Life*, she shared them with me, and since that day I noticed the progress of this virtue in her soul. She said people bothered her only when they came at odd hours, or even troubled her needlessly during her work. Whenever she was asked for some service, she always did it immediately.

"To make a service wait, to promise it for later, means not to fulfill perfect charity," she used to say to me.

> She had such a great availability that I really noticed the Sisters who abused her, demanding her help as if she owed it to them. This went so far that I was sometimes shocked, but she found it totally normal and her charity gave her the ingenuity to please the whole world. When the feast of Mother Prioress approached, almost all the Sisters brought Thérèse their feastday presents because they wanted her to decorate them with some pictures. Everyone wanted to be served first and instead of being grateful, they often criticized her: "You did Sr. so-and-so's work better; you did hers first... ," etc. Some of them demanded very complicated pictures. Thérèse exhausted herself to make them happy, but it rarely happened. All these failures seemed not to bother her at all:

"When you work for God," she said, *"you don't expect gratitude from a creature, and her reproaches can't take away the soul's peace."*[113]

---

[113] CRM 38-39.

The discernment of the novice mistress

Marie of the Trinity especially appreciated the discretion with which Thérèse treated the intimate things she had to say:

> She never asked a curious or embarrassing question, even on the pretext of doing me good. She listened to my confidentialities with interest, but never induced them. I took good note of what she wrote in her *Life*:

"When I speak with a novice, I strive to mortify myself, I avoid addressing questions to her that would satisfy my curiosity, because it seems to me that no good can come of self-seeking."[114]

When the subject matter was more difficult, Thérèse turned to the mediation of the Blessed Virgin:

> When I had my counseling session with her and had things that were more difficult to say, she brought me over to the miraculous statue that had smiled at her in her childhood and said to me:

"It's not to me that you are going to say what burdens you, but to the Holy Virgin."

> I carried this out, and Thérèse heard what I said. After this, she had me kiss Mary's hand and gave me her advice.[115]

Thérèse also asked the Virgin to inspire her counseling:

> Quite often I thought that she had the gift of reading my soul, so well did her advice correspond to the secret needs of my soul. I told her this and she said to me:

"I don't have this gift at all, but here is my secret: I never make

---

[114] C 32 v; CRM 49.
[115] CRM 13.

any remarks to you without calling upon the Blessed Virgin. I ask her to inspire me to say what would help you the most. After that, I admit that I'm often surprised myself at some of the things I say to you without there being any reflection on my part. I feel only that I am not mistaken in saying it and that it is God's will that I tell you these things."[116]

The conduct of the novices towards Mother Marie de Gonzague

We have already seen that Thérèse found herself in a very delicate position. Although she was in charge of the novices, she could not show any real authority because Mother Marie de Gonzague remained officially the mistress of novices and made sure that her little "troop" felt that clearly every now and then. One could predict the orders and counter-orders that would succeed each other... and the irritable reactions that resulted among the novices.

The novices were particularly edified by Thérèse's conduct in this same situation, and Marie of the Trinity made herself an echo of that admiration. Far from throwing oil on the fire, Thérèse always encouraged the novices to regard their prioress with the eyes of faith and to speak about her with respect:

Sr. Thérèse reproved me when I began to criticize her conduct or call her "the wolf," a nickname that we gave her among the novices.

"That was okay when she wasn't prioress, but now when she is vested with authority, we have to respect her. When we act toward her with a spirit of faith, God will never allow us to make a mistake.

---

[116] CRM 88. In the Bishop's Process, Marie of the Trinity spoke about this gift of "reading souls," referring to her difficult adjustment to the Carmel of Lisieux. The event thus dates from her postulancy or novitiate.

Even without her own knowledge, she will always give us a divinely inspired answer."

It was animated by these supernatural feelings that, encountering me one day on my way to see Mother Marie de Gonzague, she said to me:

"Did you think to pray, to commend yourself to God? That is very important in order that you may be disposed to hear Mother Prioress's words as the expression of divine will. Otherwise, you're wasting your time."[117]

This spirit of faith and respect did not prevent Thérèse from objecting to a project of her prioress which seemed to her clearly unjust. We know that Mother Marie de Gonzague had received news that the profession of Marie of the Trinity would be after the elections in March 1896; this came at a moment when she was hoping to be reelected... [in which case she would be the one to receive their vows.] For this same reason, she wanted to obtain a delay on the profession of Sr. Geneviève. Thérèse strongly opposed this new delay, which she thought was totally unjustified. One gray day in the laundry room, in January 1896, about fifteen Carmelites were doing the wash. A discussion came up about the profession of Sr. Geneviève. Sr. Aimée of Jesus, one of the strongest opponents of "the Martin clan," declared:

"Mother Marie de Gonzague has indeed the right to test her, why are you astonished?"

"There are some trials that should not be given!" Thérèse answered quite sharply.

"She made me think of our Lord when he rebuked the vendors in the Temple [cf. Mt 21:12-13]. I admired her courage," Marie of the Trinity said later.[118]

---

[117] CRM 6-7.
[118] CRM 57-58.

Moreover, Thérèse advised the others to pray for Mother Marie de Gonzague's conversion:

"It causes me more pain to see God being offended by her than to see my little Mother suffer."[119]

But the final word always belongs to the action of grace:

"The humiliations (that I underwent during the mental illness of my father) are today my glory. It's going to be the same for the humiliations to which Mother Agnes is being subjected. God will allow the good to be extracted from this hardship. Our little Mother is a saint: that's why he doesn't spare her… Surely in heaven she will have the martyrs' crown."[120]

Let us not forget to appreciate, ourselves, the discernment of Mother Marie de Gonzague that was evidenced in her day, in being the first to recognize the maturity of the youngest Martin sister. She deserves the credit for having received her into Carmel at the age of fifteen, and eight years later to have officially entrusted to her the care of the novices. Sr. Marie of the Trinity testified that Mother Marie de Gonzague expressed this thought to her several times: "If a prioress were to be chosen from the whole community, I would unhesitatingly choose Sr. Thérèse of the Child Jesus, in spite of her young age. She is perfect in everything; her only fault is to have her three sisters with her."[121]

To spend her heaven doing good on earth

Marie of the Trinity had heard Thérèse confide to her several times her hope *"to spend her heaven doing good on earth."*

---

[119] CRM 59.
[120] CRM 59.
[121] CRM 97.

In her last recreational composition, written in February of 1897, she made St. Stanislaus Kostka her mouthpiece to express her own thoughts on this subject:

"What I liked best about composing this piece is that I have expressed my certainty that after death one can still work on earth for the salvation of souls. St. Stanislaus, who died so young, has always admirably served me to say my own thoughts and feelings on this subject."

Another time, when I was looking up at the sky, I said to Sr. Thérèse of the Child Jesus: "How happy we will be when we are up there!"

— *"It's true,"* she replied, *"but as far as I'm concerned, if I want to go to heaven soon, don't think it is to rest myself! I want to spend my heaven doing good on earth until the end of time. Only then will I enjoy it and take my rest. If I did not firmly believe that my desire can be realized, I would rather not die and go on living till the end of time, in order to save more souls."*[122]

I had the impression that she had a revelation of her future glory. About this subject, she told me one day:

"My desires are mounting to infinity... What God has in store for me after my death, the glory and love I foresee, so greatly exceed everything that can be conceived, that sometimes I am forced to stop thinking. It makes me so dizzy..."

And she added laughing:

"Someone other than you would take me for a fool or a very arrogant person!"[123]

---

[122] CRM 92.
[123] CRM 94.

CHAPTER THREE

Secrets of a Heroic Joy

We have seen above that Marie of the Trinity spent many hours in copying in her regular handwriting long passages from John Chrysostom or from Bernard of Clairvaux. She liked to garner from these spiritual authors what would nourish her spiritual life. Nevertheless, for her prayers and for leading her life, it usually sufficed for her to remember the words and example of the very one she had the grace to be so close to:

> "Often," she explained to Sr. Germaine, "my prayer is simple and short, in the way Thérèse did it. I ask God to embrace you with his Spirit of love and to grant you the grace to love him more."[1]
>
> "My memories of Thérèse," she wrote to her another time, "suffice me for my prayer and I know that God asks nothing other from me than to walk the 'Little Way' on which she guided my first steps. I do everything I can not to swerve from it; it is so easy to make a detour that you have to pay special attention in order to stay on it. But when I do, what peace!"[2]

Moreover, we find in her writings and in her sayings the same expressions as Thérèse: *Papa-le-bon-Dieu* [Papa the good God], *Maman-Marie* [Mama Mary]. In her prayer she loved to slowly go over one of Thérèse's poems. When she awoke, she repeated one of her prayers.[3]

---

[1] 7/17/09.
[2] 5/28/11.
[3] 3/23/41.

Not to be appalled by one's miserable condition

Thérèse often repeated to the novices that they should not waste their time lamenting their weaknesses, but rather that they should hasten into the arms of Jesus to let themselves be purified by his infinite mercy. Thérèse, the benjamin of the novitiate, had learned this lesson well. It became the most important lesson for Marie of the Trinity, because she remained very susceptible for a long time. On November 2, 1914, she explained herself to Mother Agnes:

> "I feel only my misery and my powerlessness, I see only darkness yet, in spite of everything, I remain in an inexpressible peace. Jesus sleeps; Mary, too. I don't seek to wake them, and like Thérèse I peacefully await the shores of heaven."

Obviously there is no question of resigning oneself to one's imperfections! To walk on the "Little Way" means to run on the path of love. But to run without trying to perform in a certain way, nor to become paralyzed by the memory of one's failures:

> "You see," she explained to Sr. Germaine, "the way to be happy on the 'Little Way' of Thérèse is to abandon yourself to God and to think of yourself as little as possible, not even to seek keeping an account of whether you make progress or not. That's not our business. We have only to try to perform all the little acts of daily life with the greatest possible love, to recognize humbly but without sadness, our thousand imperfections which are always resurfacing and to ask God with confidence to transform them into love."[4]

From the other side of the confessional grille, Fr. Prou had assured Thérèse that her faults didn't hurt Jesus — an assurance

---

[4] 5/29/17.

that had overwhelmed her with joy. Strengthened by this teaching, Marie of the Trinity wanted the same certainty to be born in the heart of Sr. Germaine:

> "Ah! if you would live with me, how encouraged you would be to verify that we are both absolutely equal in our little faults. I say 'little' because at the moment we recognize them and desire to correct them, they aren't vast and they don't hurt Jesus because they serve us much more like the step of a ladder to attain to him through sufferings and humiliations. A saint is someone who always picks herself up. I don't know, anymore, who said this word, but to always pick yourself up supposes that you are always falling!"[5]

An accent which recalls the resolution Thérèse had made on the day of her First Communion: *"I will never let myself be discouraged."*

Some months later, Marie of the Trinity returned to this subject:

> "There is a very big mistake in your letter, and it is necessary to correct it as fast as possible, because Thérèse would never have tolerated it. You say: 'It's so sad to continuously hurt our beloved Jesus.' Never do the little souls like ours, filled with good will, hurt Jesus! [...] Oh! how this truth gladdens the soul! Even in this life the soul is made to taste an anticipation of heaven. I am asking my little Thérèse to make you understand this."[6]

But also, we must not forget the purifying value of the temptations that we undergo. Far from tarnishing our soul, they can make them shine with a much brighter gloss, similar — says Thérèse — to the paste that you put on copper to make it shine.

---

[5] 9/6/09.
[6] 4/3/10.

In this same sense, Fr. Pichon had said during a retreat preached at Carmel in 1907: "Each temptation leaves in the soul a gleam of beauty from the opposite virtue to this temptation." — "A thought that did me a lot of good," wrote Marie of the Trinity.[7]

To love God as much as Thérèse did

Thérèse once said to her confessor that she desired *"to become a saint, to love Jesus as much as St. Teresa of Avila, her patron."* Thérèse's disciple walks in her footsteps. In knowing herself to be truly small, through her very close relationship to the one whom Pius XI was going to canonize two months later, Marie of the Trinity made bold to write to Mother Agnes on March 10, 1926:

> "I long to love God like our little Thérèse loved him, to be the joy of his heart like she was!"[8]

This audacity does sound properly Thérèsian! Marie of the Trinity had understood the message of confidence that the pope was now preparing to sanction by canonizing Thérèse. Yes, the "role-model of holiness" that God presents to us in her is totally "accessible," Marie of the Trinity wrote one year later.[9]

Love in little things

It is a holiness that comes alive in the living of each day. We remember the magnificent synopsis that Marie of the Trinity gave in 1910:

> "I really think that this is the first time since the creation

---

[7] 9/6/09.

[8] She had already written the following to her on June 15, 1918: "Ask him, beloved mama, whether I love him here below as much as his little Thérèse loved him."

[9] 5/8/25.

of the world that someone is being canonized a saint who has done nothing extraordinary: no ecstasies, no revelations, no mortifications which easily frighten little souls like ours. Her whole life can be summed up in one word: she loved God in all the ordinary actions of the common life, performing them with great faithfulness. She always had a great serenity of soul, whether in her suffering or in her joyfulness, because she took everything as coming from God."[10]

But Marie of the Trinity wasn't forgetting the heroism with which Thérèse lived this desire to love God in all things. She wanted to let herself be trained by her example. Like Thérèse she didn't think she could climb the "steps" of perfection by her own strength: the arms of Jesus are the "elevator" that will transport her to the top. But at the foot of the stairs, while she waited for the elevator, she didn't forget to multiply her acts of love. She wanted to accomplish them "playfully," because it is always important to delight the heart of God.

"On Sundays," she said, "we play checkers. Jesus plays the white pawns, which represent grace, and I play the black pawns, which represent my nature. Each 'check' that I receive to my nature makes Jesus my vanquisher: there are many black pawns conquered by grace. In the evening examen [reflection on one's thoughts and conduct that day], we figure out together the victories and the defeats. When Jesus has won everything, our happiness is unequaled!"[11]

The joy of loving

The former novice remembered above all the insistence with which Thérèse came back to the task of being happy in all

---

[10] Germaine, 5/25/10.
[11] Germaine, 5/17/08.

circumstances. One day when she was meditating on the pages of the *Story of a Soul* relative to fraternal charity, she suddenly thought about the motto adopted by a particular saint: "To suffer everything from others and never to make them suffer." But, she said immediately:

> "To suffer everything from others isn't happiness! To get up every morning with this perspective wouldn't suit me at all. I implored little Thérèse and Mother Marie of the Angels to make clear to me what God really wants from me. Also I thought it would be pretty silly to want to suffer from others like this. On the contrary, it's necessary to resolve never to suffer from anyone. To do like Thérèse did. For example, when one Sister's chatter [lit: noise] wore her out, she would listen to it with pleasure and offer it to Jesus as a melody. Ever since practicing this resolution, I've never been so happy in my life."[12]

The terrible trial of her health did not prevent the Carmelite from already tasting here below something of the joy of heaven:

> "I already feel in my soul a breath of the eternal feast," she wrote to Mother Agnes on March 13, 1928, as if she were already very close. "It is a peace so delicious that I could truly sing from morning till night. It is not a passing peace, but the possession of an enduring joy that makes me want to say about everything that happens to me, the happy and the painful things: 'You overwhelm me with joy, O Lord, by everything you do.' Or even better, in the words of our beloved saint: *'I can't suffer anymore, because all suffering is sweet to me in the will of Jesus.'* Oh! when you believe in the love of the One who makes or permits everything for our good fortune, how happy you are!"

The ill Sr. Marie of the Trinity lived this heroic joy until

---

[12] Germaine, 4/3/10.

her death. On June 8, 1941, she admitted to Mother Agnes that she was suffering too much to still taste the joys of earthly feasts. But she corrected herself right away:

> "The truth is that I live in a perpetual feast, because of my abandonment to the will of God. I love my share just as it is, because it was given to me by God and it pleases him like this."

Several months earlier, on February 20, she had written to Fr. Marie-Bernard:

> "I am no longer content with *Amen*, but I say — willingly — *Alleluia*, and I want my life to be a perpetual thanksgiving, in spite of the huge tile that has fallen on my head!"

To suffer without courage

Fortunately there is no need to carry one's cross with "courage" in order to please God. Her friend Thérèse has sufficiently repeated this. Also, when the former novice was tempted to become desolate in experiencing her weakness, Thérèse undertook to put her back on the "Little Way." One day when Marie of the Trinity was blaming herself for not resembling Thérèse enough in her suffering, she began to pray for the gift of that love. Voilà! the next day (August 6, 1940), during the Mass of the Transfiguration — a feast on which it has been the custom at Carmel since 1895, to celebrate the Holy Face — Marie understood that her desire had made her depart from the "Little Way" and that it would be more profitable to accept to be always "poor and without courage":

> "Can you ask a little child to love suffering? She cries, she is unhappy during her suffering. [...] God likes to

hear us say with Jesus: 'Father, allow this chalice to pass from me' [Mt 26:39], because he knows that we are nevertheless abandoning ourselves to his will! I spoke to you many times about this profound grace that has done me so much good! There is nothing new in what I am telling you, but when God gives us his grace, it is luminous and transforming. Here I am at square one with my disease, but with an inexpressible joy!"[13]

To suffer one minute at a time

This peace rooted itself in the certainty that the Lord gives his strength gradually as he permits the prolongation of suffering in our lives. The sick Marie of the Trinity had a very vivid experience of this one day:

"Saturday, after the session with the doctor, God made me feel very clearly that it was He who was supporting me while I submitted myself to the torture.[14] I thought with sweetness that it was his divine hand that conducted the doctor's and that he measured the intensity of the pain to the strength he would give me to bear it. [...] I was moved to tears by this, but I dried them quickly because Sr. Madeleine came back to bandage me and she could have thought that it was the pain that made me cry."[15]

Thus the sick nun remained very little in the hands of her God, receiving everything from him:

"What sweetness I taste in the lights that God throws on my little nothingness:[16] I can't express this; it has to

---

[13] Agnes, 8/6/40.

[14] Lit.: *pointes de feu*, the same cauterizing remedy with needles that Thérèse had experienced (trans.).

[15] See CJ 18.8.4.

[16] See LT 197; Agnes, 4/14/31.

be experienced. The other day during my thanksgiving, this word: 'The extremes meet,' overwhelmed me with joy. Yes, he is our everything in proportion to our nothingness."[17]

To save the world

The Christian who suffers knows that he is not alone. He is freed forever from the pain of suffering "for nothing": his wounds are a source of grace for all mankind.

"This word of the prophet: 'The Lord wounds only to heal' [Hos 6:1], helps me a lot when I think of my lupus. Yes, all our wounds — physical or moral — united with those of Jesus, serve to heal souls. What a grace to be thus associated in his redemption!"[18]

In the image of the Holy Face

And beyond this, how could the ill Marie forget that she participated closely in redemption, when her "leprous" face was conforming her more and more to the Suffering Servant in Isaiah, to the adorable Face that she had venerated from her childhood! One day in December 1936, she saw herself in a dream next to Thérèse in the midst of venerating several different representations of the Holy Face that were hung about Carmel in different places. This dream, she explained to Mother Agnes the next morning, "left me a grace of strength to bear my illness."[19]

This mysterious resemblance to come, the Lord had in some way presaged thirty years earlier to the one then named

---

[17] Agnes, 3/13/27.
[18] Agnes, 4/29/34.
[19] 12/13/36.

"Sr. Marie-Agnes of the Holy Face." One day she said to her-self:

> "The holy image shows the head of Christ, but where
> is his body?" And the Lord seemed to say to her: "My
> body is you!" "Yes," she wrote on April 3, 1910, "we are
> the members of this adorable head. How then can we
> be astonished to experience suffering, misunderstand-
> ing and humiliation?"[20]

On September 26, 1917, remembering the desire to suffer
that had increased in Thérèse's heart after her First Communion, Marie of the Trinity wrote to Mother Agnes:

> "Suffering makes me fear. This is what makes me think
> that the Lord will spare me from it. But on the other
> hand, I feel myself so abandoned to him that he could
> do an about-turn and give me a lot. [...] What does it
> matter! I will fear nothing, I will let myself be guided
> by Thérèse, with my eyes closed, utterly honored if she
> leads me by the paths that she has taken."

In his mercy the Lord was going ahead of his spouse in
the trial that she will undergo later on. How true is this good
Thérèsian doctrine, coming straight from John of the Cross: God
always makes us desire what he will one day give to us. In con-
fiding to Fr. Marie-Bernard on July 21, 1941, that the progress
of her illness permitted her to eat only with great difficulty, the
sick nun added:

> "God gives me the grace not to be apprehensive about
> the future. I abandon myself to him like a child to the
> best of fathers who acts for the best. My great consola-
> tion is to regard the sorrowful face of Jesus and ascer-
> tain some traits of resemblance with it. Sr. Thérèse of
> the Child Jesus often loved to remind me of these words

---

[20] Germaine, 4/3/10.

of Isaiah: "He is without beauty and renown, he has nothing to attract the eye and we have despised him," etc. [Is 52:2-3]. I have been wondering about her insistence of always coming back to this same subject. Now I truly believe that God inspired her in order to tell me these things that would do me so much good later on."

The sweet presence of Thérèse

Marie of the Trinity walked the way of the cross in the memory of Thérèse, in the consolation of having worked to serve her Cause and in the astonishment of seeing her radiance spread all over the world. But there was her in heart, above all, the certainty that Thérèse was present, very close, as she had promised her: *"When I have departed,"* she had said, *"don't believe that I will be content to think about you in heaven. No, I will come down."*[21] Thérèse was truly "the radiant star in her life, the joy of her soul."[22]

This presence was sometimes granted to Marie by a delicious fragrance that all of a sudden invaded the place where she found herself. So, on May 21, 1910, she detected the very strong aroma of incense invading the room where Mother Agnes had deposited the abundant incoming mail, a heavenly perfume that lasted close to ten minutes. Marie of the Trinity saw this as a gift that Thérèse was sending for her feast: it was, in fact, the day before Trinity Sunday. She also saw this as an encouragement to respond with love to this huge amount of mail.

But, faithful to the teaching that she had received from Thérèse herself, she never considered this privilege as a sign of a greater love from heaven. She explained this to Sr. Germaine:

"I almost regret having told you this. I'm afraid that you might think Thérèse loves you less because you haven't

---

[21] CJ 7.13.3.
[22] Agnes, 2/22/31.

received all these favors, but it's completely to the contrary! I'm quite convinced, in fact, that if I had been
stronger, less beaten down, Thérèse would never have
done that and it is more of a consternation to me to see
that my imperfection almost forces her to grant me this
favor. These kinds of graces are never granted on earth
as a reward for virtue but only as an encouragement.
Here below, the reward for virtue, the proof of God's
contentment with us, is trial, temptation, sufferings of
all kinds.... Ah! how you deceive yourself to want to
believe otherwise!"[23]

Marie of the Trinity again benefitted from that kind of favor at the end of her life. In April 1940, she agreed to change
the date of her retreat in order to please another Sister. While
she was walking in the cloister near the door to choir, she joy-
fully offered this sacrifice to the Lord. Immediately, she was
surrounded with such an intense perfume of violets that she
thought it filled the whole courtyard. On August 23, 1942, after
the last bandaging session of the day, which was rendered more
painful that evening as the result of an unexpected hemorrhage
at the neck, all of a sudden she felt herself enveloped by the smell
of incense. "I thought immediately that little Thérèse had come
to tell me: 'I'm not abandoning you, I'm watching over you.'"[24]

To help the scatterer of roses

More important than the odor of roses or incense is the
shower of roses that Thérèse is pouring out upon the world. And
we must help her with this task. Marie of the Trinity encouraged Sr. Germaine to do so:

---

[23] 5/25/10.

[24] The French allows us to note a remarkable change in the relationship between
these two friends. Whereas on earth Thérèse had addressed Marie of the
Trinity with the customary formal form of the pronoun for "you" (*vous*), now
she uses the personal forms *tu* and *toi* (trans.).

"Thérèse told me that after her death we must often fill her hands with roses in order to give her the joy of being able to spread them all over the world. Thus, by our little acts of virtue, our bursts of love, we can help fulfill her most ardent desire."[25]

An unchangeable confidence

If our prayers are not granted, above all don't see this as a sign that Thérèse has forgotten us:

"I thank her always for everything, convinced that she always works for the good. My two little sisters Violette and Marguerite-Marie are always failing the exams for telegraph employment, yet they need to get a job. Thérèse knows all this, that's enough for me; I'm not worried about anything."

And Marie of the Trinity reminded herself that Thérèse did not prevent the degradation of the health of her spiritual brother Fr. Belliére. "No, Thérèse doesn't spare her true friends," she concluded, "she rather allows them to be engraved in the image of Jesus."

An outlook full of hope

On May 21, 1917, Marie of the Trinity had a dream: three Carmelites of the monastery who had died several years earlier "in the odor of sanctity," appeared to her and confirmed her in the idea that she should never be discouraged at the sight of her imperfections.[26] This dream helped her a great deal. In see-

---

[25] 5/3/08.

[26] Mother Marie-Agnes of the Child Jesus (1881-1909), Mother Isabelle of the Sacred Heart (1882-1914) and Mother Thérèse of the Eucharist (1885-1915).

ing "as in a flash of lightning" the happiness that awaited her, she began to be less afraid of suffering. She also understood that she should, with a contemplative regard, look upon and value her Sisters as already being "in glory."[27] Instead of letting herself be downcast about them because of their mediocrity, it sufficed never to forget that they could be, in an instant, transfigured by the radiant glance [le regard] of Jesus, like stained-glass windows which appear pretty dull when not exposed to the sun, but are resplendent with beauty when filled with sunlight.

Christian hope more and more penetrated the Carmelite's heart: "When Christ appears, then we will appear with him in glory" (Col 3:4). Marie of the Trinity understood better and better what Thérèse was singing: this transfiguration that will happen in our entire being when we will be given to contemplate forever the Holy Face of the Lord and to hear his Voice:

> "Oh! what a moment! what inexpressible happiness,
> When I will hear the sweet sound of your voice,
> When I will see in your adorable Face
> Divine brilliance for the first time!...
>
> In heaven, always intoxicated with tenderness,
> I will love you without measure and without laws
> And my happiness will seem to me endless
> As new as the first time!"[28]

---

[27] Agnes, 6/26/17.
[28] PN 33. "What I will soon see for the first time."

Conclusion

The spiritual itinerary of Marie of the Trinity gives the clearest lie to all who imagine that God calls to the contemplative life only those with particularly calm and composed temperaments. Her exuberant nature didn't prevent her from staying nearly fifty years in the Lisieux cloister without leaving it for one single day, even to go to vote — women's vote did not yet exist at this time!

The fervent disciple of a saint, Marie of the Trinity didn't imitate her in a servile fashion. We have seen the very personal manner in which Thérèse's former novice internalized her guide's lessons. How true it is that on the "Little Way" of confidence and love, each person can walk with her own rhythm and in an original style.

Being with Thérèse, the novice had particularly understood that joy is one of the first-fruits of the Spirit, as the apostle Paul says (Gal 5:22). *Allegremente![1]* Philip Neri liked to repeat, and we know the joyful — even playful — atmosphere which characterized the meetings of his disciples at the Oratory. This was an atmosphere similar to what Sr. Thérèse of the Child Jesus wanted to see reigning in the novitiate which had been entrusted to her. Like Teresa of Avila, she was convinced that, far from impeding union with God, such an ambience would favor it.

In line with the great spiritual tradition, Thérèse spotted the importance of the warfare that needs to be carried out against the disease that the ancients denounced under the name

---

[1] Briskly, joyously, merrily! (trans.).

acedia, which we today readily call "moroseness."[2] Already in the second century, the *Shepherd* of Hermas had denounced the noxious effects of this harmful sadness: "Every joyful person acts well, thinks right and tramples sadness underfoot. The sad person, on the contrary, always acts badly: first of all, he acts badly by saddening the Holy Spirit who is given to mankind as joy; second, he commits an impiety in not praying to the Lord, because the prayer of the sad person doesn't have the strength to mount up to the altar of God. Sadness mixed with prayer prevents it from rising, like vinegar mixed with wine takes away its taste. Purify your heart of harmful sadness, then, and you will live for God."[3]

For Thérèse, joy was above all one of the privileged ways of expressing her love to God. It was one very simple way for us to tell him how much we appreciate his infinite tenderness and mercy and that we don't blame him for the sufferings whose presence he permits in our lives as pilgrims.

Furthermore, this joy is a foretaste of the unmixed happiness into which we are invited to plunge at the hour of our death. Are we not invited to participate here on earth, in the wedding feast of the lamb [cf. Rev 19:7]? Then, as Madeleine Delbrêl later sang: why not live our whole life as a dance?

> Teach us, Lord, to put on anew every day
> Our human condition
> Like a ball gown, that makes us love about you
> All its small details like indispensable jewelry.
>
> Make us live our lives
> Not like a game of checkers, where everything is
>   calculated,
> Not like a sports match, where everything is difficult,

---

[2] *Acedia* is usually left in its Latin form, but means apathy or indifference, of which moroseness (*morosité*) is an effect (trans.).

[3] [French] translation by Olivier Clement, in *Sources,* Stock, 1982, p. 149.

Not like a theory that breaks our head,
But like a feast without end
Where the encounter with you is being renewed
Like a ball,
Like a dance,
In the arms of your grace,
To the universal music of love![4]

Thérèse insisted on the necessity of having the expression on her face be in accord with the profound joy in her soul. But she didn't forget that the smile of the whole face [*le regard*] and of the lips can coexist with the sufferings of a sick body and the disappointments of a wounded heart. Sr. Thérèse of the Child Jesus of the Holy Face always remembered the vigorous advice she had received from Fr. Pichon and which, at the age of sixteen, she transmitted to her sister Céline:

"Don't think that we can love without suffering, without suffering a lot. Let us suffer with distress, that is to say, without courage!... Jesus suffered with sadness; can the soul suffer without sadness? And we would like to suffer generously, grandly. [...] Céline! ... What an illusion!"[5]

Certainly we don't always live our trials with this evangelical serenity. Marie of the Trinity knew this better than anyone. But Thérèse had taught her the art of not dwelling on her weaknesses and the audacity to offer herself constantly to the consuming Fire of God's mercy.

"We are not among the saints who are weeping over our sins: we are delighted with everything that serves to glorify the mercy of God." — "One can never have too much confidence in God, who is so

---

[4] *Nous autres, gens des rues* ("The rest of us, people of the streets"), Seuil, 1996, pp. 91-92. For more on Madeleine Delbrêl (1904-1964), see Charles F. Mann, *Madeleine Delbrêl: A Life Beyond Boundaries*, San Francisco, New World Press, 1996.
[5] LT 89.

powerful and so merciful! One receives from him quite as much as one hopes for!" (see pp. 75 and 77).

O happy weaknesses of the novice without which we would never have harvested these Thérèsian "pearls"!

Let us underline, finally, the simplicity with which Marie of the Trinity has told us about her memories of Thérèse. Very much aware of the privilege that she had, to live so intimately close to her for three years, she never used it to glorify herself. She never took herself too seriously. Never do we see her priding herself on having known "the greatest saint of modern times" and on having been one of her most beloved novices. She was quite content to hand over her memories to us, even when the anecdote didn't always show the novice at her best! Above all, she made the effort to follow the counsels she had received, and we have seen the heroism with which she did it.

But like Thérèse, Marie of the Trinity would scold us if we would be exaggeratedly enraptured before this heroism. *"I still didn't have one minute of patience. It isn't my own patience!... You're always wrong about that!"*[6] Thérèse protested on August 18, 1897, a day when she heard one of her sisters voicing her admiration for her.

> On her part, Marie of the Trinity said one day when Dr. Maffei had casually admired her, "How that good doctor exaggerates! If he could judge things truthfully, he would see that God alone deserves the praises, because it is his grace that works in us and gives us the strength to suffer what he asks of us."[7]

Yes, Marie of the Trinity always retained the disposition of a child. A child "doesn't do evil things," a child is intensely aware of her radical incapacity to get out of it all by herself! And

---

[6] CJ 8.18.4.
[7] Agnes, 2/7/41.

when she falls into faults or sin, she doesn't "make a fuss" about her foolishness; she throws herself into her Father's arms, certain of being immediately pardoned.[8]

Blessed be the Lord for having guided to the Carmel of Lisieux in 1894, the young Marie-Louise in the enthusiasm of her twenty years of age! She didn't use her knowledge of stenography to record the words of her novice mistress, but she kept in her heart the living example which she had before her eyes, astonished that it had pleased the Lord to grant her one of her desires from childhood: to have a saint as a friend!

Thanks to her testimony, Marie of the Trinity's privilege could become our own: we, too, can go to the school of Thérèse and we, too, can have a saint as our friend! And we will say as she did: "No! life is not sad!"

---

[8] Cf. LT 258 (trans.).

Testimonial Documents

Marie of the Trinity knew Thérèse for only three years. But she lived in such intimate closeness to her that, right away, her testimony was considered particularly precious.

A) FIVE SERIES OF DOCUMENTS

In view of the publication of the *Story of a Soul*, the novices were invited immediately after Thérèse's death to put in writing the examples and words that they had retained of their former mistress. Then they were asked to add the reception of favors that they had obtained through her intercession; in other words, to be more specific about how Thérèse had helped them to understand and live the "Little Way." These notes have not been kept, but they permitted the drafting of the first four documents indicated here below.

1. Counsels and Reminiscences *from the* Story of a Soul *(CSM)*

At the end of 1898, Fr. Godefroy Madelaine, who supervised the second edition of the *Story of a Soul*, advised Mother Agnes to condense chapter twelve concerning the last days and the death of Thérèse and to add under the title *Paillettes d'or* ["Flakes of Gold"] some stories drawn from the novices' memories. "Don't put in anything mediocre," he wrote to the prioress. "There are enough very beautiful things. Or else, beware:

the blue pencil (of the censor) will be at work."[1] That is why Mother Agnes inserted thirteen of Marie of the Trinity's recollections in the 1898 edition, whereas she had only two in the first edition.

The 1907 edition accorded an even more important place to the recollections of the novice. A special section entitled *Counsels and Reminiscences* replaced the *Paillettes d'or* of the previous editions and this time contained thirty entries of Sr. Marie of the Trinity — a contribution that takes up more than a third of the section. Her name was still not mentioned but it's very easy for us to recognize the stories concerning her.[2]

2. *The deposition in the Bishop's Process (PO)*

When the novices brought their testimony about Thérèse before the ecclesiastical tribunal that was convoked by the bishop of Bayeux, Marie of the Trinity quite naturally used the notes that she had composed twelve years earlier, the main part of which had already appeared in the succeeding editions of the *Story of a Soul*.

Marie of the Trinity had been "facing" the ecclesiastical tribunal for several hours on March 13, 1911, when one of the judges interrupted her to obtain a clarification. The question was meant to be embarrassing: "How is it that your testimony corresponds word for word with the published text in the *Story of a Soul* under the title *Counsels and Reminiscences*?" The witness explained: "What was included in the complete edition of the *Story of a Soul* under the title *Counsels and Reminiscences* was taken for the most part from the notes that I myself wrote down

---

[1] Letter of 12/3/1898.

[2] In a letter dated August 12, 1908, she indicates to Sr. Germaine Leconte about twenty stories which concern her in the 1907 edition. Why doesn't she speak about the other ten? We don't know. But we easily find them in the depositions she made later in the course of the two Processes.

according to my recollections and which I am using afresh for my deposition."[3]

Her depositions in the Bishop's Process contain many more sayings and episodes in the life of Thérèse that still hadn't found a place in the 1907 edition of the *Story of a Soul*.

3. *The* Red Notebook *(CRM)*

Five years had passed since the information-gathering Process had started. The Carmelite of Lisieux had brilliantly passed her tests in the heart of Rome. On June 10, 1914, Pius X signed the introduction of her Cause: a second Process now had to conduct the investigation, led by the delegation of the Holy See: the Apostolic Process. It took place in two principal stages: the opening Process in Lisieux (sessions 3-58, from April 9, 1915 to August 25, 1916), giving priority "to the aged and ill witnesses," and to those who were likely to be leaving the diocese; and the continuing Process, likewise in Lisieux for the most part (sessions 59-60, from September 22, 1916 to October 6, 1917). The final, very solemn session took place at the cathedral of Bayeux on October 30, 1917.

Marie of the Trinity was the first witness in the second part of the Process (September 22-28, 1916), in reality the twenty-first witness in the Apostolic Process. She was also the most important witness, by far, in this second group.

The Carmelites had carefully prepared their testimony, as can be verified by consulting, in the archives of the Carmel of Lisieux, the hundreds of pages — large format or school notebook — of the *Notes preparatoires au proces apostolique* [Preparatory Notes for the Apostolic Process] (NPPA).[4]

---

[3] PO, p. 454.

[4] We can read the description of these manuscripts in DE, pp. 833-840. We find here, for example, the rough autographs that Mother Agnes had composed in 1915, very probably reusing her preparatory notes for the Process in 1910. But we find here also a copy of those notes by Sr. Madeleine of St. Joseph, which were continued by Sr. Marie of the Trinity in 1933.

Why don't we find here the notes of Marie of the Trinity? Because she herself went to the trouble to rewrite them later — most likely in 1932-1933.[5] She put together one copy that takes up 149 pages of a red-covered notebook (21 x 13.5 cm.), which is commonly called the *Red Notebook*. Once this work was done, she destroyed all of the previous drafts.

The format of the *Red Notebook* is the same as for the depositions of all the witnesses at the Process. The witnesses say how the Servant of God lived in a heroic way the three theological virtues (faith, hope, love of God, love of neighbor), the four cardinal virtues (prudence, justice, fortitude, temperance), her three religious vows (obedience, poverty, chastity) and humility. In the end, it is a question of her supernatural gifts, her reputation for holiness during her life, her death and her reputation for holiness after her death.

4. *The deposition in the Apostolic Process (PA)*

Although the *Red Notebook* is entitled: "Deposition of Sr. Marie of the Trinity and of the Holy Face for the Apostolic Process regarding the Servant of God Thérèse of the Child Jesus and of the Holy Face, September 23-30, 1916," there is nothing identical between the *Red Notebook* and the official text of the Apostolic Process.

After having read their "Preparatory Notes" before the tribunal, the Carmelites in fact gave their texts back to M. Dubosq. He indicated with a mark in the margin what he thought ought to be kept intact in the text (continuous red line), what needed to be summarized (wavy red line) and what could

---

[5] In a note dated March 5, 1933, Sr. Marie of the Trinity actually proposed to Mother Agnes to take back the copy of her deposition for the Apostolic Process (see note 4). In order to disentangle such unreadable scribble, it is quite probable that she was going to do it by hand, recopying her own deposition.

be omitted (blue mark).[6] This explains, for example, the attenuations in the official answers of the Apostolic Process: the phrases which the vice-postulator had found exaggerated but which Marie of the Trinity conserved in the *Red Notebook*. This indicates its prime importance.

5. *To these four documents is added another series of* Counsels and Reminiscences *which can be gleaned from the papers of Marie of the Trinity or from the writings concerning her. An issue of* Vie thérèsienne *printed a regrouping of twenty-seven of them (CSM 31-57).*[7]

Differing from the first thirty *Counsels and Reminiscences* published in the 1907 edition of the *Story of a Soul*, these didn't have a "public" destination. The Carmelite transcribed them for her own personal benefit on loose sheets of paper and, without doubt, in the notebooks which have since been destroyed. Most frequently she would offer these texts to Mother Agnes as a spiritual bouquet for her retreat. They also allowed her to satisfy the eagerness of a correspondent who was particularly enthusiastic about Thérèse [Sr. Germaine]. In the meanwhile, Marie of the Trinity was not unaware that some day or other these confidential writings could be utilized — it wouldn't be only for the writing of her own obituary letter — which in fact came to pass.

---

[6] These pencil marks made by M. Dubosq can still be seen on the NPPA which are kept in the Lisieux Carmel archives. A number sometimes indicates that, for the benefit of the whole impression, the devil's advocate has transferred an answer from one questioner to the other.

[7] VT 77. Here are the sources of this new series of *Counsels and Reminiscences*: seven remarks come from the loose sheets; thirteen are borrowed from the notes written to Mother Agnes, of which sixty-six have been conserved; three are gathered from a packet of letters addressed to Sr. Germaine, of the Carmel of Angers; one, written in verse, comes from a small notebook of poems written by Sr. Marie of the Trinity between 1896 and 1942; two others are quoted from the obituary letter of Sr. Marie of the Trinity; a final one is drafted according to an event given in the very latest edition of the *Story of a Soul* (1953).

B) THE VALUE OF THE WITNESS

Three remarks deserve to be made:

— *We are dealing here with notes written after the fact*, according to memories all dating from the years 1894-1897. The delay in transcription varies from several weeks to several years after Thérèse's death. Their accuracy can't be compared to those of the *Last Conversations* that Mother Agnes recorded for the most part, day by day, sometimes even "on the fly."

— *The possible editorial intervention of Mother Agnes* (the one in charge of the first editions of the *Story of a Soul*) *has to be reckoned with*. The Sisters gave her their notes, and she harmonized the style of the ensemble. We are correct in supposing that her intervention was restrained in the present case. Marie of the Trinity had a lively pen and a gift for "flashy" picturesque expressions which rightly make her entries interesting. Her notes would have required only a minimum of "touching up."

She then compared her work with the printed text of the *Story of a Soul*. If, in the *Red Notebook*, she sometimes modified the presentation of facts — in order to clarify a detail — she almost never touched the words of Thérèse.[8]

The last series of *Counsels and Reminiscences*, alone, seems to have allowed a more elaborated presentation of Thérèse's sayings. But the circumspect style with which Marie told her stories was in perfect conformity to Thérèse's simplicity, instead of trying to reproduce her sayings word for word.

— *Concerning the essentials, the witness is reliable.* "Young and attentive, she sees and remembers rapidly. The carefree nature of her character is counterbalanced by 'her interest in her subject,' for all those things coming from an elder Sister whom she admires, and a friend whose influence she accepts without reservation. Emotionality and imagination can blur objectivity, it is true. And above all, an opportunism, not always praisewor-

---

[8] Sr. Cécile, VT 73, pp. 53-54.

thy, would be the flip side of a Norman finesse taken to extremes."[9] Marie of the Trinity was, for example, one of the most severe regarding Mother Marie de Gonzague, as the *Red Notebook* testifies, while in her notes to Mother Agnes she doesn't hesitate to use intentional exaggeration to express her affection.

C) DATING OF THE REMINISCENCES

"She who ought to have been one of the first to establish a chronology of the saint, and who for many long years was the editor of the calendar, has left us wanting as to the dating of her recollections. 'One day... In one circumstance'! It is really vague!"[10]

Nevertheless, the comparison of the vocabulary with those of the writings, the indication of a community event, sometimes permits a dating of the entry. On the other hand, we can reasonably suppose that all the genuine "confidential exchanges" between Thérèse and her novice took place only from the moment when their friendship became so deep (1896-1897).

Finally, let us not forget that the witness was separated from the sick Thérèse beginning in June 1897.

Given the impossibility in this work to date in a precise manner the greater part of Marie of the Trinity's memories about

---

[9] Idem., p. 54.

[10] Idem., p. 54.

[11] "In his book, *Thérèse of Lisieux, the Saint of Spiritual Childhood* (Lethielleux, 1980, p. 25), Fr. Philip of the Trinity has given us a precious account of the interview he had with Sr. Marie of the Trinity in 1940:

"She was already more than sixty-five years old, but carried her years courageously despite the lupus that she suffered in half of her face (covered by a white veil). She gave me an impression of holiness and simplicity that I will never forget. She spoke to me about St. Thérèse with an *affectionate* and *respectful* veneration that still moves me. I also remember her half-veiled face bathed in a wholly spiritual light.

"Here is what I wrote down of what she shared with me in the course of our conversation:

Thérèse,[11] we have preferred to rearrange the material by themes, following a specifically Thérèsian logic.

"Sr. Thérèse of the Child Jesus would have been asleep during prayer if she hadn't 'pricked' her Gospel book. During the summer we had six hours of sleep at night, plus a nap after lunch. She was trying to hold on, but she was falling forward during Mass, falling from tiredness. She slept almost all the way through her thanksgiving, kneeling, head on the floor. She couldn't prevent it.

"With a milder prioress and some normal concessions, she would have held up. She was strong but young. The weather was terribly cold the year of Sr. Geneviève's profession.

"She wouldn't have said to herself, 'I won't read at prayer,' and she wouldn't have read at any time.

"One day she said: *'My cheeks hurt from laughing so much.'* One day she came with a little foot warmer and said: *'This will be the world upside down: the saints have entered heaven with their instruments of penance, I will enter with my foot warmer.'*

"She said to me: *'Even though you are a very bad girl, you will not go to purgatory !'*"

CHRONOLOGY OF THE LIFE OF SISTER MARIE OF THE TRINITY

Before Her Entrance into Carmel

1874	August 12	Birth of Marie-Louise Castel, St. Pierre-sur-Dives (Calvados), the 13th of 19 children
	August 13	Baptism
		With a wet nurse until she was four years old
1882		Family moves to Paris
		She attends school run by the Daughters of the Cross
1885	May 21	First Communion and Confirmation; Thérèse Martin renews her First Communion in Lisieux
1890	May	She consecrates herself to God by making a private vow of virginity
		Pentecost: interview with the prioress of the Carmel of *l'avenue de Messine*
		Retreat with Fr. Blino, SJ, who spoke about Sr. Thérèse
	August 12	16th birthday

At the Paris Carmel

1891	April 30	Entrance into the Paris Carmel under the name Sr. Marie-Agnes
1892	May 12	Taking of the habit
	Dec. 9-16	Retreat given by Fr. Boulanger, provincial OP
1893	July 8	Leaves the Carmel for reasons of health
		Sojourn on the Norman coast
		Visit to the Lisieux Carmel where she meets Mother Agnes of Jesus (prioress) and Mother Marie de Gonzague (novice mistress)

At the Lisieux Carmel

1894	June 16	She enters the Lisieux Carmel under the name Sr. Marie-Agnes of the Holy Face; Sr. Thérèse of the Child Jesus is her "angel"
	June 24	Sr. Thérèse affirms that the novice "has enough voice for both of them"; beginning of their friendship
	Dec. 18	Taking of the habit, a second time; Thérèse composes a poem for her, *"Finally the time of tears is over"*
1895		Her profession is postponed
	Dec. 1	Makes her Oblation to Merciful Love, 1st Sunday of Advent

1896	March 6	Name is changed to Sr. Marie of the Trinity and of the Holy Face
	March 21	Mother Marie de Gonzague is reelected prioress; Thérèse is officially in charge of the novitiate as assistant novice mistress, teaches her "Little Way"
	April 30	Profession of vows; Thérèse composes two more poems
	May 7	Taking of the Veil; Thérèse gives her 3 texts from St. John of the Cross
	May 31	Trinity Sunday Feast-day gift of another poem by Thérèse, *"I am thirsty for love"*
	Autumn	Crisis of her possible departure for the Carmel in Saigon
	Christmas	Gift of the spinning top
1897	Spring	Thérèse's health dangerously declines; Marie of the Trinity is removed as assistant infirmarian for fear of contagion
	August 12	Thérèse writes her a "final goodbye" note for her 23rd birthday
	Sept. 30	Death of Thérèse

After the Death of Thérèse

1901		"The rogue of Carmel" at age 27
1902		Beginning of her composition of the Gospel Concordance, which she completes on January 21, 1903
1903	May	Visit of Fr. Thomas Taylor to Carmel, who initiates the idea of a canonization
1904		Recopying of her eight most important dreams since childhood
	September	Dream about Thérèse and the night of faith
1905	June 6	Pius X beatifies the 16 Carmelites of the Revolution and Carmel receives the Tournai seminary's petition for the cause of Thérèse
		Influx of applicants to the Carmel of Lisieux
1908		Correspondence begins with the Carmel of Angers, through Sr. Germaine Leconte, which extends over 6 years
1909		Mail numbers 20-30 letters a day
1910		Writing of her deposition
		Msgr. de Teil calls her the "Mother-archivist"
	May 21	"Feast day gift" from Thérèse: a strong smell of incense on this day before Trinity Sunday

	August 3	Opening of the first canonical Process
	September	Exhumation of Thérèse's coffin; fragrance of roses from wooden debris
1911		Mail increases to 50 letters a day
1911	March	Entrance of her youngest sister Marguerite-Marie, who leaves four months later
	Mar. 13-15	Deposition in the Bishop's Process
	Dec. 12	Beatification Process ends in Bayeux
1912	January 29	Marguerite-Marie enters the Visitation in Caen under the name Sr. Marguerite-Agnes
	Dec. 12	"Devilish hubbub" in choir
	Dec. 13	Newspapers publish Vatican approval of Thérèse's writings
1913		Bishop-pilgrims come from all over the world
	October 1	Mme. Castel and Michaëlle become custodians at *Les Buissonets*
1914		Mail increases to 400 letters a day
1915	June 23	Death of Mme. Castel
1916	Sept. 22-28	Deposition in the Apostolic Process
1917	May 21	Dream about the 3 holy Carmelites of Lisieux
1923-1925		Mail is 600-1000 letters a day
1923	February	Marie of the Trinity has pneumonia and lupus begins on the back of her head
	March 26	Solemn transference of the relics of Thérèse; Marie remembers Thérèse's prophetic dream about this day
	Nov. 23	Fr. Daniel Brottier becomes director for the Work of the Orphans-Apprentices of Auteuil; novena to Blessed Thérèse; friendship begins with Marie of the Trinity
1925	May 17	Canonization of St. Thérèse of Lisieux
1928		Marie's death seems near
1941		Her illness worsens; bandaging takes 2 hours
1942	August 12	Hemorrhaging at the neck, following her bandaging session; smell of incense is Thérèse's gift for her 58th birthday
1943	Dec. 8	Lupus jumps to her heel
1944	January	Community epidemic of flu; Marie of the Trinity gets the worst of it
	January 15	Last Sacraments and final words
	January 16	Death of Sr. Marie of the Trinity and of the Holy Face
	January 19	Burial in the town cemetery